GW01607682

SECRETS OF THE ALCHEMISTS

MYSTERIES OF THE UNKNOWN

SECRETS OF THE ALCHEMISTS

By the Editors of Time-Life Books

TIME-LIFE BOOKS, AMSTERDAM

CONTENTS

GOLD

The metal is so rare hat if every grain aken from the earth ince time began vere melted into a ingle cube, it would neasure less than nineteen yards to a ide. No civilization has attained great- ness without it; its oss has toppled empires. Yet since humans first beheld he metal's entranc- ng shimmer and

A sun ablaze with gold leaf hung in medieval Munich's town hall.

associated it with the life-giving sun, gold has been treasured far beyond its value as the medium of wealth and power. It is the metal of gods, fashioned by virtually all cultures into their most revered objects.

Artifacts like the ones here manifest enlightenment, purity, and immortality. To the alchemists, who sought to create gold from baser matter, their highest aim was not mere riches, but divinity itself.

A death mask found in a royal grave at the Greek citadel town of Mycenae gleams as brightly as it did in the sixteenth century BC, when it was hammered out of a paper-thin sheet of solid gold. Because gold does not rust, tarnish, or decay, it has long symbolized incorruptibility and immortality.

This tiny scarab, small enough to be mounted on a ring, was modeled after a dung beetle by an Egyptian goldsmith more than 3,000 years ago. The ancient Egyptians came to associate the beetle with the daily appearance and disappearance of the sun. Thus to them, the scarab was a symbol of rebirth; rendering it in immutable gold reinforced the insect's symbolic connection to everlasting life.

This gem-studded chalice, commissioned in late-tenth-century France by the bishop of Toul, was used to celebrate the Eucharist. In that sacrament, Christians seek union with God through symbolic consumption of the Body and Blood of Christ. The golden sheen suggested purity, as befitted a cup that would contain the Divine Presence.

This small, gilded Buddha from the powerful Tang dynasty of eighth-century China reflects the reverence accorded gold by the Buddhists of eastern Asia. They saw the natural radiance of the precious metal as a manifestation of supernatural omnipotence and eternal spiritual values.

Symbolizing the priestly powers of a shaman, this figure was cast and hammered smooth by a Tolima Indian craftsman centuries before the Spanish conquest of Colombia. Called a pectoral, it was worn on the breast to represent the shaman's flight to the kingdom of the sun god; the gold used to create it was prized for its ability to reflect the brilliance of sunlight.

Hundreds of tiny gold spangles held by fine wires shimmer like glistening confetti on this 2,000-year-old crown, once worn by the princess of a nomadic tribe on the Bactrian plain of northern Afghanistan. Featherweight and crafted so that it could be taken apart and packed flat in a saddlebag, the headpiece was an ingeniously portable token of its wearer's wealth and rank.

CHAPTER 1

Chasing the Seductive Gleam

Few citizens of seventeenth-century Holland were more esteemed for their wisdom and scholarship than John Frederick Schweitzer, better known as Helvetius. Court physician to Prince William of Orange and author of many learned tracts, he epitomized the spirit of rational inquiry then on the rise in Europe. The scientific giants of the time—Johannes Kepler, Robert Boyle, and Isaac Newton—were forging a new understanding of nature and casting doubt on the complicated web of myths and superstitions that had helped earlier generations cope with their lack of logical explanations. In a quieter way, Helvetius had been doing his part to bring light to the field of medicine. Among his accomplishments was the exposure of certain ineffectual popular patent medications, or "sympathetic powders." In the process, he suggested that much of the accepted lore on magic—the grand arcanum of the sages—had to be regarded with skepticism. But one day, as Helvetius later related, he was given cause to wonder.

On a bleak December afternoon in 1666, a stranger knocked at his door in The Hague. The visitor was a grave and sober-looking man—dark-haired, beardless, and clad in the simple garb of a Mennonite pastor. He began immediately to quiz the learned doctor, trying to poke holes in his dismissive views on magic. Was there in fact no universal medicine, no grand elixir such as the one the sages had reported? And what about the fabled philosophers' stone, a substance so charged with mystical potential that it could transform lesser metals into gold?

Helvetius conceded that a universal medicine would be most desirable, but he assured his guest that he had never uncovered one and doubted that it was a possibility. As for the philosophers' stone, he had scoured a great many texts of arcane wisdom and had never found reason to believe that the miraculous material existed.

At this, the visitor drew from his pocket a handsome ivory box. Inside were three transparent, yellowish crystals about the size of small walnuts. Taking one in his hand, Helvetius was struck by the material's surprising weight and wondered at its sulfurous glow. Could this be the miraculous substance of legend?

Helvetius asked his visitor if he was a student of medicine, but the man only shook his head. He was an artist and a brass founder, the stranger replied, although he had learned many unusual things in the study of alchemy and knew how to extract certain medicines from metal. While Helvetius was examining the crystal, the man told him a little about its wondrous properties—its power to heal, to extend life, and to transmute base metals. "You are holding enough of the tincture," he asserted, "to produce twenty tons of gold."

Helvetius's curiosity was piqued, and he begged for a tiny fragment of the crystal—even if it was no larger than a coriander seed. The stranger refused, insisting that he would be violating his principles if he was to give away the smallest trace of the precious commodity. Helvetius would not let the matter drop, however, and he led the way into a lavishly furnished inner chamber.

When they had settled comfortably, Helvetius's visitor asked to be shown some small item of gold for purposes of comparison. He then drew back his vest to reveal five shiny saucer-size pendants. He had made all this gold himself, the man declared, using but a speck of the very crystal that Helvetius was holding. Now Helvetius turned insistent, and after a great deal of prodding, he finally persuaded the stranger to come back in three weeks to show him how the goldmaking was accomplished.

The days that followed were an agony of anticipation for Helvetius. To fill the time, he carried out a small experiment. While examining the alchemist's crystal, he had managed to appropriate a few tiny crumbs by scraping them off with his fingernail. These he now sprinkled into a crucible that contained molten lead. Much to his disappointment, however, he was rewarded not with gold but only a chunk of glassy earth. Frustrated, he wondered if he had been played for a fool.

On the appointed day, the stranger again appeared at Helvetius's door. There ensued a lengthy discussion on the marvels of nature and the peculiar traditions of alchemy. But although the doctor pleaded and fussed, his visitor was reluctant to offer a practical demonstration. Then he seemed to relent. Cutting off a snippet of his alleged philosophers' stone, he handed the prize to Helvetius and announced: "Receive this small parcel of the greatest treasure in the world, which truly few kings or princes have ever seen or known."

"But this perhaps will not transmute four grains of lead," the doctor protested. He knew, because he had already attempted to do exactly that. Helvetius then told his visitor about the failed experiment. The man let out a short laugh. "You are more dexterous at committing theft than applying the tincture," he replied. "If you had only wrapped it in yellow wax, to preserve it from the fumes of the lead, it would have sunk to the bottom and transmuted it into gold. The violence of the vapor, partly by its sympathetic alliance, carried the tincture quite away."

This explanation sounded somewhat hollow to Helvetius, and he began to suspect that his visitor was a fraud. The next day, however, he decided to attempt the transmutation again. Firing up his laboratory furnace, he melted half an ounce of lead—an amount the stranger had suggested. His wife, meanwhile, coated the particle of crystal with yellow wax. When the lead began to flow freely, Helvetius dropped in the wax-covered stone. And by his account of the event, a miracle occurred.

The mixture in the crucible bubbled and hissed, then glowed with astonishing iridescence, as though it had captured a rainbow at the source. It turned a brilliant green and then, as Helvetius poured the preparation out to cool, it changed again—taking on, he wrote to a friend, "the lively fresh color of blood." Within fifteen minutes, Helvetius reported, the mixture had hardened into an ingot of "the best and finest gold." A visit to the town assayer confirmed the outcome of the procedure—or so Helvetius maintained.

The seductive gleam of gold has captured the imagination of people like Helvetius since the dawn of human consciousness. One of very few metallic elements to occur free in nature, uncombined with other elements, it washes down the beds of streams, glimmers from the sides of cliffs, and snakes in shimmering veins through bedrock like the roots of some exotic plant. About 40,000 years ago, in what is now Spain, Paleolithic cave dwellers gathered bits of the metal and hoarded them in their caverns. Sparkling brightly, the nuggets must have seemed like condensed motes of sunshine. The inhabitants of ancient Peru certainly thought of gold that way: To the Incas it was "the sweat of the sun," used to make everything from fishhooks to ceremonial tiaras. To Hindu sages it was "the mineral light," a physical token of divine intelligence. And the Greek poet Pindar, writing in the fifth century BC, called it "the child of Zeus." Even today, gold's chemical symbol, Au, derives from the Latin word for "shining dawn."

No wonder, with this divine provenance, that gold has always carried an aura of mystical power. Because it does not tarnish, it was held to be the most worthy of metals—pure and incorruptible, an enduring symbol of all that was good and perfect. Even touching it was thought to bestow benefits. Some Chinese monarchs ate their meals from gold plates, believing that the practice would give them eternal life—or at least extend their time on earth. The Roman naturalist Pliny the Elder took a more circumspect view; nevertheless, he recommended gold ointment as a cure for everything from ulcers to hemorrhoids.

Throughout long stretches of history, the search for gold was jealously guarded as a royal monopoly. Even before the first gold coins were struck—at Lydia in Asia Minor during the seventh century BC—the pharaohs of Egypt were extracting the metal from the sands of the Nile. They had it cast into jewelry or pounded into sheets to adorn their palaces and temples. Every Egyptian ruler, no matter how brief his reign, wound up in a tomb outfitted with a dazzling assortment of gold furnishings and utensils for use in the afterlife. One

Dutch physician Helvetius, looking here the very essence of conservative judgment, was convinced he had actually transmuted lead into "the most excellent gold in the world."

monarch, Queen Hatshepsut, who lived around 1500 BC, was so captivated by the metal that she made a habit of powdering her cheeks with the dust of electrum, a silver and gold alloy.

Most of the pharaohs' gold was extracted from two enormous deposits of mineral-laden quartz in the deserts flanking the Nile. One deposit was in Nubia, which sprawled to the south in what is today the Sudan. The name of the region was derived from *nub,* the Egyptian word for "gold." The other deposit, in Upper Egypt, spread east through a sun-blasted plateau between the Nile and the Red Sea. Together they contain the oldest gold mines on earth, dating back some 5,000 years.

At the cost of much blood and anguish, the pharaohs' hard-driven slaves bought their masters greater riches than humankind had ever known. As much as 1.4 million pounds of gold was plucked from the desert, making Egypt the wealthiest and most powerful nation on earth.

The ancient world had other sources of the metal—in Spain, Anatolia, Arabia, East Africa, India, and elsewhere. But every ounce taken from the ground only fired the appetite for more. Merchants traded for it, princes went to war for it, and increasingly, through the ages, kings and commoners alike solicited the aid of supernatural agencies to obtain it.

Thus it was that men like Helvetius toiled in laboratories and libraries, searching for the divinely granted ingredient that would transmute ordinary matter into the most noble of metals. They puzzled over dusty manuscripts and huddled before smoke-belching furnaces, stirring up sulfurous powders and evil-smelling potions. Often, they sacrificed health and fortune in the course of this work. And over time the search itself underwent a strange transformation. What had begun as a quest for riches changed gradually—at least for some—into a journey of the spirit. The work of the alchemist began to reach into the highest levels of philosophical inquiry; if gold was matter in its perfect form—a metallic sunshine, an offspring of the gods—then any person who learned to create it would certainly take on the attributes of divinity. The successful alchemist would be wise, powerful, and quite possibly immortal.

The transformation began at the heart of the ancient world's gold supply in the sun-drenched lands of the Nile basin, and it stemmed from the impressively sophisticated skills developed by the metalsmiths of Egypt. Although the jewelers and goldsmiths of that civilization often doubled as temple priests and court officials, they were craftsmen first—not philosophers. What concerned them most were the physical properties of gold and the techniques for making use of those qualities. They learned to exploit the extraordinary malleability of the metal, hammering it into intricate designs, pounding it into diaphanous sheets, and drawing it into decorative threads as thin as human hairs. The Egyptians also mastered the art of refining gold, as well as other metals, because the gold from their mines was seldom entirely pure. The product of the Nubian excavations, for example, contained a large component of silver, giving it a slightly greenish cast. Other samples had a reddish tinge, from traces of copper. To turn these alloys into pure, 24-carat gold, metalworkers had to heat the ore in combination with various chemical fluxes, which would combine with the impurities and draw them away.

For most purposes, however, pure gold was too soft to be useful. So the Egyptian goldsmiths learned to make their own alloys, mixing in traces of silver, copper, and other metals. These adulterants added strength and also imparted characteristic hues, which altered the decorative effects of the gold. One favorite alloy was produced with iron, which gave the gold a rich purplish sheen. Some of the precious metal found in Egyptian tombs contained so much iron that it responded to magnetism. Other samples sparkled with visible flecks of platinum. Producing such dramatic changes in color and brilliance of gold became a straightforward matter for the master jewelers of Egypt, but to uninitiated observers in that age their powers seemed altogether astonishing.

Even more impressive was the apparent ability of goldsmiths to increase the amount of treasure in a given

In a facsimile of a 3,400-year-old tomb painting, Egyptian goldsmiths practice their already long-established craft. At top left, gold is weighed in, and at bottom left, two men carry finished work, including a collar and bracelets.

sample. By adding just the right proportions of silver and copper, for example, a craftsman could boost the volume of metal, while retaining a pure gold color. And if a goldsmith was really hard-pressed, he might concoct a bright yellow alloy using nothing but copper and zinc. Without proper light, only another expert would be able to tell that the resulting metal was not gold but brass.

As with most ancient arts, the goldsmith's skills were closely guarded trade secrets. Several instruction manuals have survived, however. One is a papyrus produced in the third century AD and now held at the University of Leiden in the Netherlands. It provides ninety recipes for various colored alloys, including artificial gold and silver. "To increase the weight of gold," reads one recipe, "mix it with a fourth part cadmia (an ash containing copper, zinc, and arsenic). It will become heavier and harder."

Many of the techniques described in the Leiden papyrus are for imparting a golden hue to metallic surfaces. The deluxe method is the one still used today—dipping the object in an amalgam of gold and mercury. But the Egyptians also had some less expensive solutions: "To gild a silver or copper vase without gold leaf, dissolve some yellow soda and some salt in water; rub this in."

A few of the recipes cited by the author of the papyrus concern not the coloring of metals but the coloring of cloth. Indeed, many Egyptian metalsmiths were also dyers, and some of the same tints and mordants used in treating textiles were pressed into service transforming the appearance of metals. Why these changes occurred the Egyptians did not ask. They were practical, not given to lofty speculation. It was sufficient that their methods worked.

In the years preceding the birth of Christ, a philosophical revolution swept the Mediterranean world, altering forever humankind's understanding of the universe—including the art of metallurgy. The seeds of change had been planted centuries earlier in the Greek-speaking cities of Ionia, in Asia Minor, where the first influential Western philosophers were questioning the nature of things. For these people, the "why" was everything. This questioning impulse reached full blossom in Athens during the fifth and fourth centuries BC, in the works of Socrates, Plato, and—particularly—Aristotle, who did the first systematic study of natural phenomena. As time progressed, the ideas of the great Greek philosophers sifted down to Egypt, where they mixed with the occult beliefs of many different Eastern traditions.

In the Nile delta, a focal point for the intermingling of philosophies was the port city of Alexandria, which had become the capital of the Ptolemaic Greeks and one of the largest metropolises of its day. With great public buildings, a distinguished university, and a library of more than 700,000 scrolls, Alexandria was known as the Queen City of the Mediterranean. For a time, it was the cultural and intellectual hub for many Greeks, Egyptians, and Jews. And as some of the prominent scholars of the city turned their attention to the metallurgical expertise of the ancient Egyptians, a new discipline took shape. The Greek philosophical outlook on the world blended with the traditional practices of goldsmiths to give birth to the art of alchemy—the science of the grand arcanum.

The story of how this cross-pollination of cultural influences developed is as mysterious as the arcanum itself. The earliest documents on alchemy have all disappeared, destroyed along with the contents of Alexandria's library in a series of conquests by the Romans, beginning in the year 47 BC. More than three centuries later, Emperor Diocletian was threatened by unrest among the Egyptians and responded by banning the practice of alchemy and burning all the texts on the subject. Presumably, he hoped to impoverish the unruly Egyptians and thus force them into submission.

Nor does it help that the alchemists of later centuries pushed back the genesis of their art to the dim and mythical past, ascribing its invention to such unlikely sources as Moses, King Solomon, and the Egyptian goddess Isis. One legendary adept—as practitioners of the art came to be called—was an Egyptian sage named Chemes, who supposedly passed on his wisdom in a book he called *Chema*. Some scholars believe that this adept's name provided the root for the word *alchemy*. Others believe the term was derived from the Egyptian word *khem*, referring to the black soil of the Nile delta, or else from the Greek word *chyma*, meaning "that which is poured or cast"—as in turning molten metal into ingots.

But the most oft-cited candidate for founding genius of alchemy was Hermes Trismegistus—or Thrice-Great Hermes—who, according to some versions of the legend, was an Egyptian priest of the first century AD. Other accounts hold that he was the human incarnation of Thoth, the god of wisdom and scribe of the underworld, who came to earth and reigned as pharaoh for 3,226 years. In this view, Thrice-Great Hermes was credited with the authorship of 36,525 books, comprising all possible human knowledge. Thoth was the inventor of writing and also gave the world mathematics,

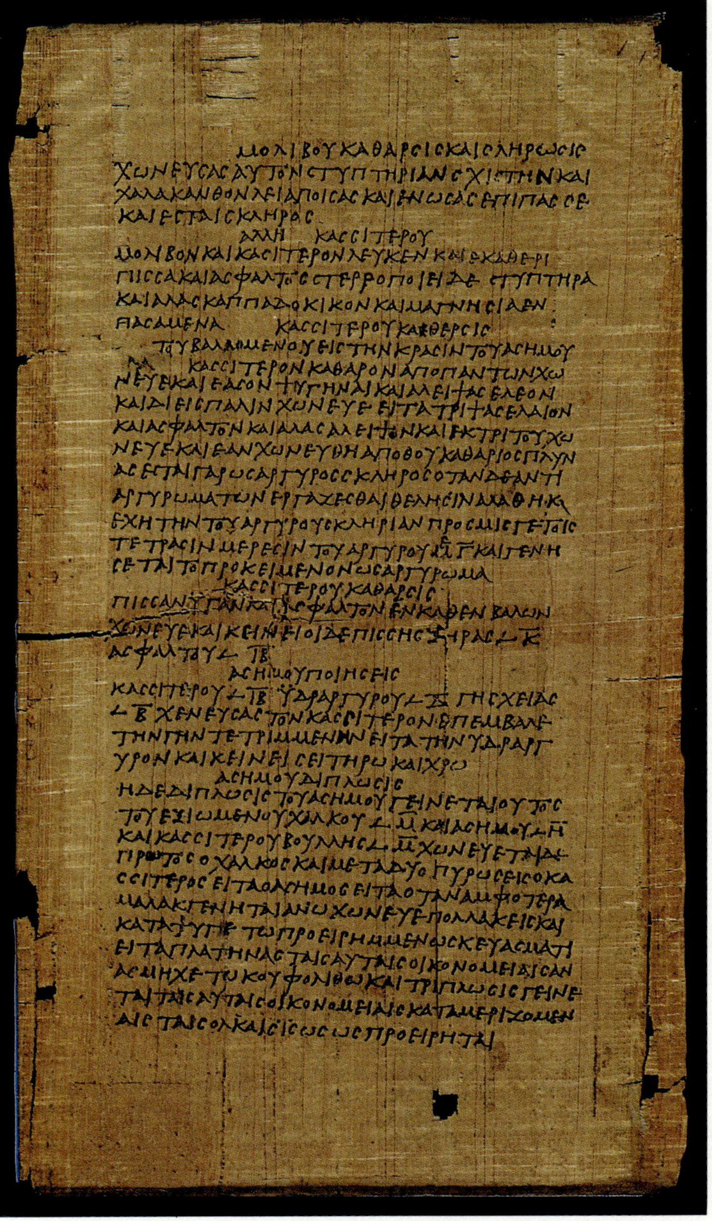

The Leiden papyrus, a third-century Egyptian manuscript, is sometimes cited as evidence of alchemy's early beginnings. It describes how to make "artificial gold" and how to expand gold by adding alloys, but it does not tell how to create genuine gold from base metals.

astronomy, medicine, and magic. When the Greeks transported Thoth into their own mythology, they equated him with the deity Hermes, messenger to the gods and patron to travelers, merchants, gamblers, thieves, and charlatans. Whatever his true identity, the alchemists embraced Hermes Trismegistus as their own, and their craft became known as the Hermetic art.

Among the works attributed to Hermes Trismegistus was an emerald tablet, long since vanished, on which he supposedly inscribed the fundamental principles of the grand arcanum. Manuscripts alleged to be transcriptions of the tablet surfaced occasionally over the centuries, and the instructions they set forth were extremely cryptic. They ran to pronouncements such as: "Just as all things proceed from One alone, by meditation on One alone, so also they are born from this one thing by adaptation." Another passage exhorted the alchemist to "separate the earth from the fire and the subtle from the gross, softly and with great prudence."

Whatever meanings these sayings may convey, they were intended to follow from the tablet's central precept: "What is below is like that which is above, and what is above is like that below." This dictum goes to the heart of several ancient philosophies and has surfaced in many forms of magic worldwide. It teaches that every aspect of the physical world in some way reflects a more fundamental reality in the world of spirit.

The assumption underlying this controlling principle was that the divine presence of the god who created the physical universe must necessarily permeate all things. Operating from this premise, the priestly astrologers of the Middle East saw a direct correspondence between the heavenly panorama of stars and planets and events here on earth. Other sages, with a more abstract turn of mind, sought out controlling intellectual principles that govern all reality. Pythagoras, a Greek philosopher of the sixth century BC, decided that the principle was mathematics, and that everything in the universe could be described in terms of numbers—a premise still asserted by many scientists today. Another Greek, Empedocles, argued a century later that all reality had sprung from the opposition of two primary forces—love and strife. Whatever the specific conclusions, the basic notion that material facts and invisible values were closely entwined was a matter of general agreement. And it was this idea that would turn many alchemists away from the simple quest for gold as material wealth in favor of a search for spiritual enrichment.

Central to progress in either direction was the task of defining the nature of matter itself. The Greek philosophers had much to say on this topic as well, for if the universe was—as they contended—a unified whole, then everything in it had to be composed of a single underlying substance. The earliest of the Ionian sages, Thales of Miletus, suggested that the primal stuff was probably water, since nothing can grow or multiply without it. Someone else proposed air, and still others suggested fire. Among the leading champions of fire was Heraclitus of Ephesus. He argued that the only certainty in the cosmos was continuous change, and that fire represented change in its most essential form.

Clearly the most intuitive analysis of this matter was put forward by the Ionian Democritus, who lived in the fifth century BC. He suggested that everything was composed of tiny particles he called atoms, from the Greek word for "indivisible." Although all atoms were composed of the same substance, some were round and slippery and thus tended to flow; these were the atoms of water. Others, Democritus suspected, had rough, jagged surfaces like the atoms in iron and therefore clung together. By this reasoning, the various types of matter resulted from the different arrangements of their constituent atoms, and one type could be transformed into another by rearranging its atomic structure.

The atomic theories of Democritus enjoyed a brief popularity, then fell into eclipse; more than twenty centuries would pass before anyone thought to revive them. Most thinkers—and later on, most alchemists—preferred a more tangible substance for the basic composition of all matter. So the three original candidates—water, air, and fire—were trundled out, along with earth, another of Empedocles' suggestions. To resolve any conflicts, Empedocles declared that all four substances were basic elements, or "roots," of matter. The materials of the physical world differed, he said, because of the numerous ways the four elements could be combined. For many centuries, the theory of the four root elements would reign supreme. It did not hurt that the two greatest minds of the classical world, Plato and Aristotle, both found the theory acceptable.

For his part, Aristotle took the hypothesis into account as he conducted a systematic study of natural phenomena. In his view of matter, the four elements did exist, but they were not really elemental because they could be converted from one into another. Heated water, for example, turned into air by forming an invisible vapor. Subjected to cold, it solidified, becoming in effect a variant of earth. Following this logic, earth, water, and air represented matter in its solid, liquid, and gaseous states, while fire could be seen as representing the principle of energy, or combustibility.

Casting the net of his logic still further, Aristotle decided that each element embodied the coupling of two basic qualities: Fire was hot and dry, earth cold and dry, water cold and wet, and air hot and fluid. By his reasoning, this accounted for the transformations he had observed. If an element traded one quality for another, it became a different substance altogether. When a fire burned down, giving up heat, it became cold and dry—earth in the form of ashes. Furthermore, two elements could merge to become a third by each discarding a superfluous quality. Thus, air and earth could ignite as fire by losing their fluidity and coolness.

Underlying these metaphysical gymnastics, Aristotle believed, was an element more basic than earth, air, water, and fire, a substance that centuries later became known by the Latin name *prima materia*, or prime matter. The prima materia was not actually matter but had the potential of becoming such, Aristotle declared, and it did so whenever one or more of the elemental qualities could be imposed upon it to give it material form.

Aristotle also had definite ideas about the origins of metals, including gold. Metals came, he suggested, from "vaporous exhalations" generated by the sun. When the sun's rays fell on dry land, the exhalations were smoky and hot, like the fumes from a volcano. These bred minerals such as galena and cuprite, ores of lead and copper. Cool, misty exhalations from bodies of water and damp ground produced gold and other similar metals. The fact that these hard substances could be melted down confirmed their watery origins—at least in Aristotle's eyes.

To the great philosopher's contemporaries, his theories went a long way toward explaining the miracles performed by the Egyptian metalworkers. The smelting of ores—a basic transmutation, and itself a wondrous process—could be seen as the art of using fire to rearrange the elemental proportions of a mineral. In a like manner, adroit readjustment of the elemental mix made it possible to "tint" base metals—to turn them into gold—and to "grow" more of the precious metal by incorporating it into an alloy.

In performing these acts, the skilled metalsmith was simply helping nature carry out its work. The prevalent belief in classical times was that gold was a living substance; it grew like carrots or truffles in the soil, warmed by the sun and nourished by the rains. Lesser metals, moreover, were thought to have a natural tendency to transmute themselves into more valuable substances. According to another of Aristotle's precepts, all of nature was—like the human race—intent on self-improvement. In his words: "Nature and God are working towards an end, striving for what is perfect." Gold, being the most nearly perfect metal, was the obvious end product of these spontaneous changes.

Among the other strains of thought that drifted into Alexandria to mix with the ideas of the classical philosophers was astrology, an import from Mesopotamia. This system confirmed the first dictum of Hermetic belief: "As above, so below." And the Mesopotamians, adroit metalsmiths themselves, had their own theories of celestial linkage. Each of the most important metals, they believed, belonged to one of the seven known planets. Lead was equated with Saturn, heavy, dull, and sluggish. Mars was iron, rust-red in color and important in warfare. Mercury,

Among the divine roles of the ibis-headed Egyptian deity Thoth—thought by some to inhabit the human body of Hermes Trismegistus, the supposed originator of alchemy—was lord of time. In one ancient inscription he was exalted as "he who exists from the beginning . . . he who rests on the truth. What he utters subsists for eternity."

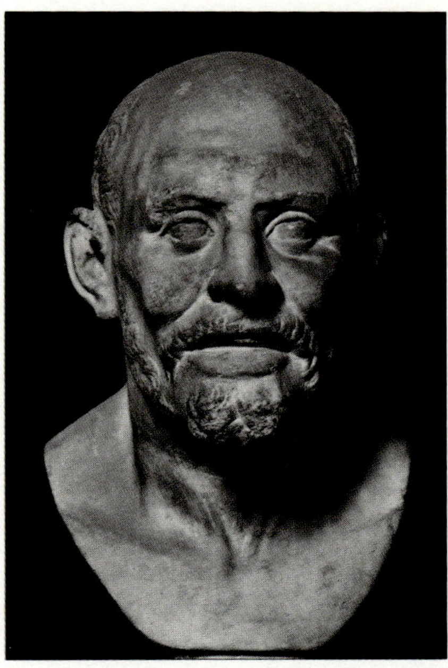

Greek philosopher Democritus, who some 2,400 years ago foreshadowed atomic theory by saying matter was composed of tiny atoms, also believed those atoms were in constant motion. The motion, he said, was eternal, but it could be changed by outside pressure. Thus, he suggested, when a vapor is condensed into a liquid, its atoms are slowed and pushed closer together. Some modern scientists see Democritus's thoughts about the movement of atoms as a primitive forerunner of a fundamental tenet of physics, the law of the conservation of motion.

slithery and quick, was associated with the planet of the same name. The Moon was silver, and the Sun, naturally, was gold. Borrowing a page from Aristotle, the Alexandrians were convinced that each planetary orb played a role in producing its corresponding metal on earth.

Another strong influence on the earliest alchemists was the great jumble of religious creeds that found expression in cosmopolitan Alexandria. In addition to followers of the native Egyptian rites and the cults of the Romans, about 40 percent of the population was Jewish, and synagogues dotted the city. Christianity also exerted its influence, sprouting a number of competing sects, and various mystery cults from the East introduced secret rituals of rebirth and purification and an orientation toward mystical union with God. Amid all these contrasting religious viewpoints, occult beliefs hung over the city like a theological smog.

Students of alchemy apparently felt free to pick and choose ideas at random from this free-floating assortment of creeds. One of the first alchemists whose name survives was Democritus of Alexandria—no relation to the Greek originator of atomic theory. Democritus lived in the first or second century AD, and later adepts have credited him with scores of texts on alchemy. In all probability, few of the manuscripts were actually his work. One of the texts that is thought to be authentic resembles the Leiden papyrus in that it consists mainly of recipes. In one of the few narrative passages, Democritus describes an incident of divine revelation in which he acquired his alchemical skills.

After some years of instruction in the theories of alchemy, Democritus was nearing the point when he would undergo initiation into the mysteries of the secret art, but his teacher, Ostanes, suddenly dropped dead. The only way to obtain the further guidance he required was to summon Ostanes back from Hades. According to Democritus, he managed to do so after a great deal of prayer and incantation. Unfortunately, Ostanes would tell him nothing.

"Grant me this gift," Democritus pleaded. "I know the diversity of matter, but how do I bring its natures into harmony?" Ostanes finally relented, but only in so far as passing on this simple message: "The books are in the temple."

Democritus and a few of his fellow students searched the temple high and low but came up empty-handed. A service of worship began, and Democritus decided to stay and attend it. Suddenly, his manuscript relates, one of the pillars of the temple opened up, and inside was an inscription: "Nature rejoices in nature; nature conquers nature; nature brings forth nature."

These words were all that Democritus required. In a flash of mystical insight, every detail of his training suddenly made perfect sense. All that he had learned about formulas for dipping copper into mercury or sprinkling base metals with arsenic, sulfur, zinc oxide, or antimony took on new logic and meaning, and Democritus became an adept.

The belief that occult knowledge of this sort leads the mind to perfection was not new with alchemy; it had been developing in Alexandria for several centuries. Certain Jewish sages saw wisdom as a medium for bringing souls to God, and the idea was incorporated into a philosophy of magic known as the Cabala. Various Christian sects espoused similar notions, which turned up in the arcane manuscripts called the Gnostic Gospels. Gnosticism—from *gnosis,* the Greek word for "knowledge"—pondered such matters as the nature of reality, the quest for the eternal, and the perpetual battle between good and evil. Its aim, like that of most mystical religions, was to free the soul from the evil confines of the material world and return it to God.

For the alchemists, this train of thought had practical significance. To obtain the perfection of gold, they reasoned, they had only to free the essence of the noble metal from the base materials that imprisoned it. Improvising makeshift laboratories, they devised a number of ingenious

The symbols scattered on these pages, each representing both a heavenly body and a metal, show how closely alchemy was linked to astrology. Alchemists believed that seven principal metals had grown like embryos inside the earth, each under the influence of one of seven known "planets"—a term that included the sun and moon. Thus the old planetary symbols were assigned to the metals.

Gold/Sun

procedures to accomplish this process of liberation.

Among the most revered of the laboratory workers was a woman referred to as Maria the Jewess. As with most early adepts, Maria's identity is now obscure. In the past, alchemists believed that she was Miriam, the sister of Moses, but there is little evidence to support this claim. More likely, she lived around the time of Democritus, in second-century Alexandria. And whatever her origins, she was a genius at designing laboratory equipment and using it in original ways. Her main contribution was an apparatus called the *kerotakis,* used for heating alchemical substances and collecting their vapors. Another of Maria's inventions, a water bath, is the same double boiler found in well-equipped kitchens today; it is still known in France as a bain-marie.

Silver/Moon

The kerotakis was an airtight vessel with a piece of copper foil suspended at the top. When the alchemists heated their various compounds of sulfur, arsenic, and mercury, the fumes would condense on the foil and the copper tended to change colors—giving the impression that it was taking on the spirit of gold. For the apparatus to function properly, all of its connections had to be vacuum tight. The use of such containers in the Hermetic arts gave rise to the expression "hermetically sealed."

Mercury/ Mercury

Maria and her colleagues thought of the reaction that took place in the kerotakis as a mystical reenactment of the process in which gold was formed within the bowels of the earth. Her favorite roasting compound was realgar, an orange-red mineral consisting of arsenic sulfide that often turns up in gold mines. And she equated the fire of her hearth with the flames of Hades, which purged every substance consigned to them. In the course of the alchemical process, the realgar was in effect "killed," leaving behind a blackish residue that the alchemists came to call the "corpse." The sulfur, meanwhile, was freed, and like a disembodied soul it wafted up to heaven.

None of Maria's writings survived in their original manuscripts, but her teachings were frequently cited by later Hermeticists. And the works of another female alchemist, who called herself Kleopatra, have endured.

Copper/Venus

The most notable fragment left behind by Kleopatra was a single page of symbolic diagrams. One of its images showed a serpent swallowing its tail to form a ring. The phrase "The One is the All" was inscribed within the circle. For centuries to come, alchemists would find no more succinct statement and symbol for their beliefs: The encompassing serpent reinforced the idea of cosmic unity, in which the world above suffused the world below and all matter was interchangeable. According to some traditions, the serpent represented a sexual union between humankind and God—or at least an ecstatic penetration by the Divine Spirit. Because snakes shed their skin, they were thought to be long-lived, perpetually renewing themselves through endless cycles of rebirth.

The cycle of death and rebirth had long been a fundamental theme of mystical religions, and it would become a recurring motif in hundreds of alchemical texts. Perhaps the greatest of the Alexandrian scholars who made reference to this cycle was Zosimus of Panopolis, a town in Upper Egypt. In about AD 300, Zosimus compiled the teachings of many earlier adepts to form what amounted to an encyclopedia of the Hermetic art.

Iron/Mars

Zosimus described a number of laboratory utensils, including the kerotakis, and he repeated the usual recipes for turning base metals into gold. He also ventured an explanation of sorts on how transmutation actually worked. To make gold, he said, the alchemist began with a substance from which all the important "qualities" described by the Greek philosophers had been symbolically removed.

Ouroboros, the serpent that bites its own tail—here depicted as a four-legged, dragonlike beast rather than a snake—represented the alchemists' belief that matter is in a constant cycle of destruction and creation. It was an enduring symbol: The serpent's earliest forebear tempted Eve with the lure of forbidden knowledge; and Gnostics would carve its tail-eating progeny on their rings and pendants.

This prima materia would be devoid of all color and thus would appear black to the eye. The alchemist then had to add the proper formative qualities in a very particular sequence and in just the right proportions, thereby advancing the prima materia upward through the scale of metallic virtues. As progress was made, it would be reflected in the color of the alchemical substance, which would change from black to grayish white, to yellow, and finally to vivid reddish gold—perfection itself. The principal catalysts applied by the alchemist were sulfur, representing the spirit of fire, and mercury, which added the spirit of fluidity.

If the final result did not always meet the standard tests for gold, Zosimus noted, the alchemist should not necessarily be discouraged. It could be that the process would have yielded something even more precious—a "coral of gold" so suffused with golden essence that it held the power to transform any other substance into the glittering metal. In a fragment of writing later attributed to him, Zosimus described a "stone which is not a stone, a precious thing which has no value, a thing of many shapes which has no shape, this unknown thing which is known of all." This may be the oldest surviving reference to what would come to be known as the philosophers' stone, a substance that alchemists of ensuing centuries would seek more avidly than gold itself.

♃

Tin/Jupiter

Over time, the writings of the Alexandrian sages became ever more theoretical and vaporous, until only a true adept could even hope to penetrate their meaning. "O matter immaterial holding matter fast . . . O golden-roofed stream of heaven, and silver-crested spirit sent forth from the sea . . ." droned the seventh-century Hermeticist Stephanos, going on interminably in that vein. Then suddenly, yet another one of history's major transformations shifted the balance of Western thought.

Fanning out from the parched sand wastes of central Arabia, where the prophet Muhammad had inflamed them with visions of religious conquest, came armies of desert tribesmen. In AD 633, the legions of Islam galloped into Syria and then to Iraq and Persia. Egypt fell in 643, followed by the rest of North Africa and the whole of Spain. Among the notable casualties was the great city of Alexandria. Its university was destroyed and its precious store of manuscripts carried off as the spoils of war. The city would decline into a dusty provincial seaport, and for the next five centuries, the serious work of scholarship in the Hermetic arts would take place in Islamic centers like Baghdad, Damascus, Córdoba, and Toledo. The most important alchemical texts during the period would be written in Arabic.

♄

Lead/Saturn

No city of the era that followed the explosive expan-

A World of Earth, Air, Fire, and Water

At the heart of the alchemists' belief that base metals could be turned into gold was the assumption that all worldly materials were composed of a few fundamental constituents. For centuries, most thinkers agreed that the basic ingredients were earth, air, fire, and water, as suggested by Empedocles and Aristotle.

Those four elements were amazingly durable in their grip on the popular imagination and down through the ages became recurrent themes in art and verse. The idealized visions here are by sixteenth-century Flemish artist Jan Brueghel, who saw the elements in terms of deities associated with them.

Less than fifty years after Brueghel completed the works, the theory of the four elements came under heavy attack from scientists and eventually was discredited. But the idea of a world in which everything is reducible to a few commonplace substances has never lost its poetic appeal.

Brueghel's depiction of the nature goddess Demeter captured the fruitfulness of earth.

Hephaestus, god of fire and the smith's forge, sits amid the ruins with a smoke-belching mountain in the background.

Wife of the sea god Poseidon and an ocean deity in her own right, Amphitrite signified the bounteous gifts of water.

To represent air, Brueghel portrayed an assembly of birds and Urania, the muse of astronomy.

κλεοπατρης χρυσοποιια

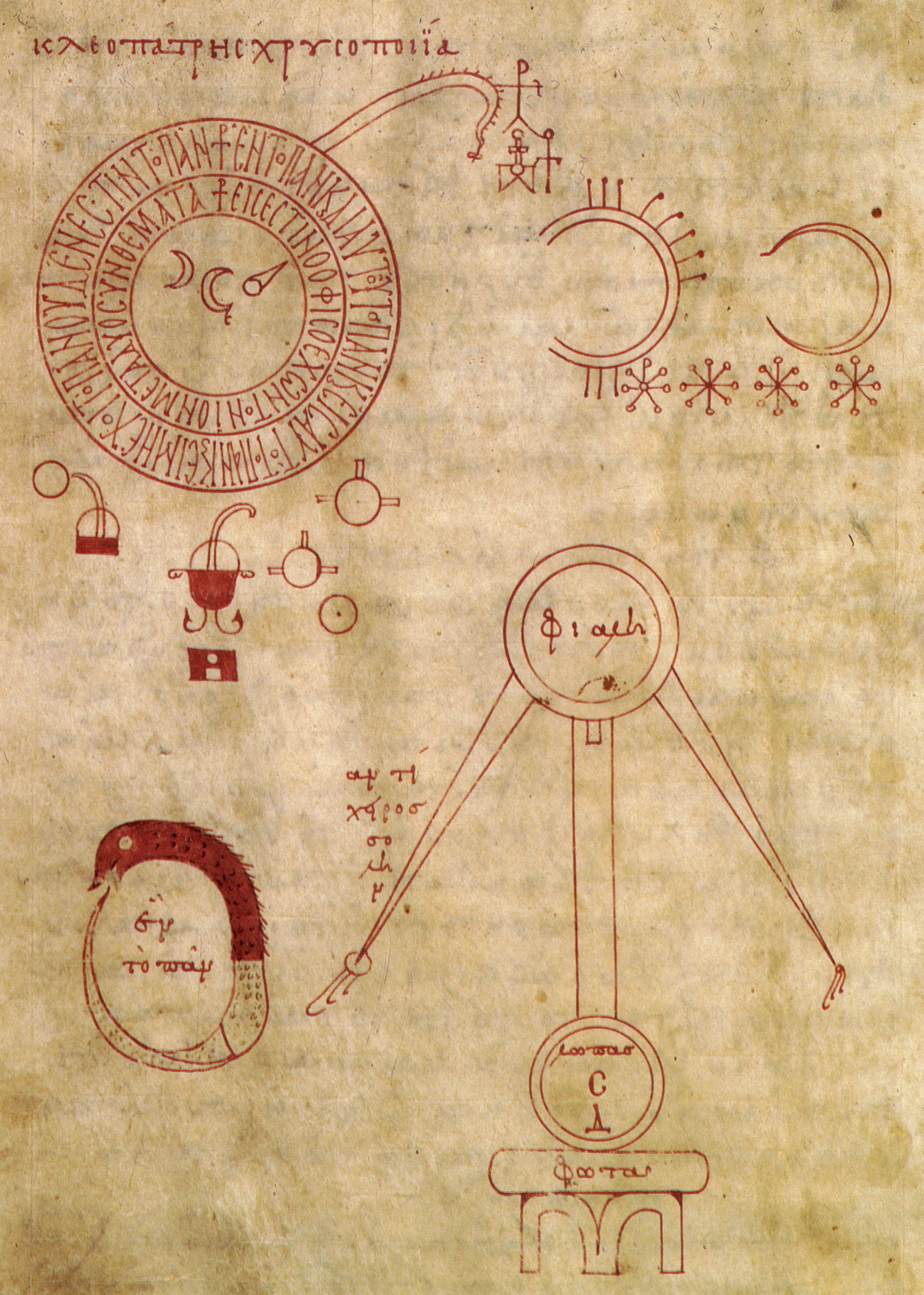

These diagrams, copied from the work of a classical alchemist called Kleopatra, were labeled "Goldmaking." Greek words in the circles at top left enigmatically declare: "One is the All and by it the All and in it the All and if it does not contain All it is nothing." At lower right an alembic, or still, sits on a furnace. At lower left is a serpent biting its tail, perhaps alchemy's most important symbol.

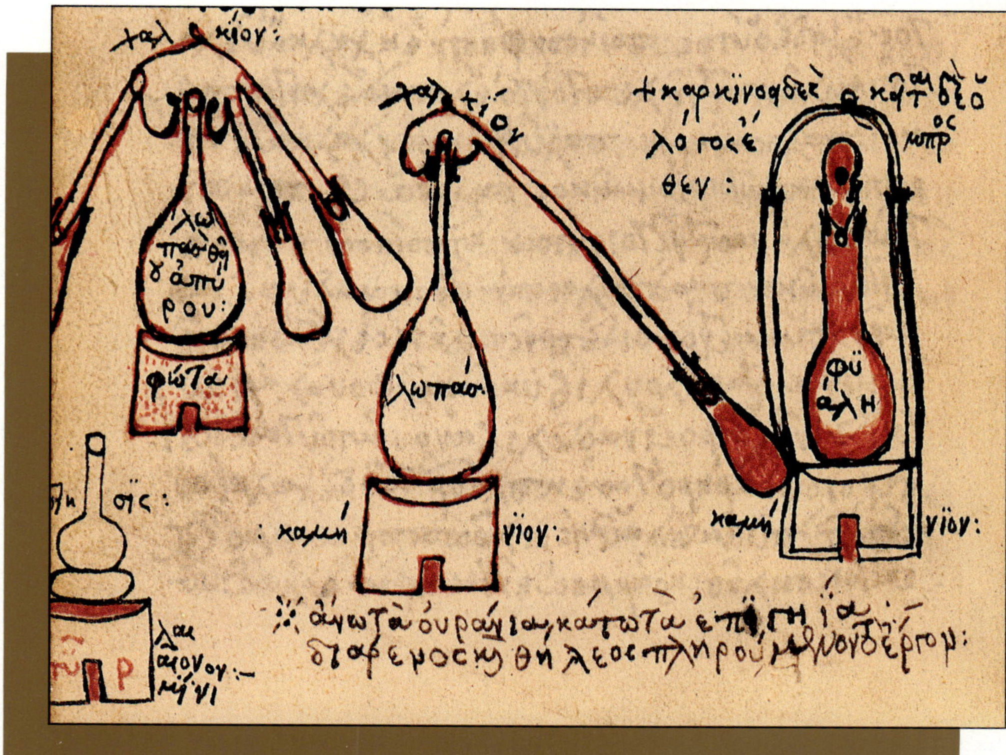

"Above, the heavenly things; below, the earthly," reads an axiom surrounded by alembics, tubes, vials, and a furnace in these drawings of alchemical laboratory apparatus. They are taken from a 1478 copy of On Instruments and Furnaces, a treatise written centuries earlier by Zosimus, the most important Greco-Egyptian alchemist.

sion of Islam was more dazzling than Baghdad, an oasis of gardens and palaces located on Iraq's Tigris River. There in the capital of the imperial Abbasid dynasty, in the latter half of the eighth century, the father of Arabic alchemy lived and worked. He was Abu Musa Jabir ibn Hayyan, court physician to the caliphs; he became known in the West as Geber.

Like many scholars of earlier times, Geber was a polymath, learned across a spectrum of disciplines ranging from medicine to music, from philosophy to military science. He had studied the writings of Plato and Aristotle and was familiar with some of the manuscripts carted from Alexandria. In the context of the writings of the Alexandrian alchemists, Geber's own ideas on the subject represented quite a departure.

When it came to gold, the Arabs were practical, having little patience for ethereal musings. Geber's response was to start with the basics, and he became the first adept since Maria the Jewess to write from the laboratory. "He who makes no experiments," he taught, "will attain nothing."

Geber's hands-on work yielded a number of new compounds that would later find a role in the as yet ill-defined science of chemistry. Mixing vitriol with alum and saltpeter, he discovered nitric acid, or *aqua fortis,* as he called it. A dose of ammonium chloride then produced something called *aqua rigia*, one of the few substances corrosive enough to dissolve gold. He is also said to have invented a luminous ink, a rust inhibitor, and a technique for waterproofing leather and cloth.

In the realm of theory, Geber elaborated on the theories of Aristotle. Whereas the great Greek philosopher taught that earthly "exhalations" generated metals and minerals, Geber taught that the process was not so direct. The smoky vapors, he believed, first became sulfur, and the misty vapors became mercury. These, in turn, were the building blocks of all metals. Innate impurities in the sulfur and mercury caused the formation of lesser metals like iron and lead. But if the alchemist could make these substances chemically pure, the result, he believed, would be gold.

Geber labored long and rewardingly in Baghdad, although there is no record that he ever succeeded in manufacturing gold. On the contrary, he cautioned his followers to count their pennies, since the study of alchemy could impoverish even a wealthy man. Unfortunately, during the reign of Harun ar-Rashid, the illustrious caliph of the *Arabian Nights,* Geber found himself on the wrong side in a bitter political squabble and ended his days in exile. He would not be the last adept to be declared an enemy of the state.

Geber's pioneering efforts launched a golden age of Arabic alchemy. The discoveries of the Islamic adepts gave the world new words such as *alcohol, alkali,* and *alembic*—the last being an apparatus used in distillation. Another contribution, *elixir*, added a new dimension to the Hermetic art. An elixir, like the philosophers' stone, would transmute base matter into gold and do much more besides. The concept was itself a borrowing from other ancient cultures. The Islamic empire, spreading east, soon stretched to the borderlands of India and China, where various occult beliefs of the Orient began to find their way into Western alchemy. Among them was the notion that a quaff of liquefied gold would impart immortality. Needless to say, a number of alchemists decided to turn their attention to the pursuit of an elixir of life.

This attempt to outfox death may account for the fact that so many practitioners of alchemy were also physicians. Rhasis of Persia was one of them. Born around 825 in the desert town of Rayy, Abu Bakr Muhammad ibn Zakariya ar Razi was in his youth a freethinking spirit devoted to music, poetry, and metaphysical philosophy. Necessity intervened, however, and at the age of thirty he moved to Baghdad to study medicine. Before long, he became caught up in the allure of alchemy.

Like Geber before him, Rhasis placed his faith in practical experimentation. His laboratory was among the most advanced of its time, fitted with the very latest in burners, forges, sand baths, steam boilers, rock crushers, slides, spatulas, beakers, crucibles, flasks, filters, funnels, vials, and retorts. All these various pieces of apparatus are described in a classic manual entitled *The Book of the Secret of Secrets*, which historians for the most part attribute to Rhasis. In addition to glorying in the details of the laboratory, the work explains many of the basic techniques of alchemy, among them calcination, sublimation, distillation, and coagulation. On the theoretical front, Rhasis's principal contribution was the original proposition that, in addition to the sulfur and mercury cited by Geber, all metals required some component of salt. This triumvirate of ingredients—mercury, salt, and sulfur—would live on for centuries in the lore of alchemy.

Eighth-century physician and scientist Geber is considered by many the greatest chemist of Islam and one of the most important alchemists. He proposed that metals were made of positive and negative principles that, once made pure, would create gold.

An even more eminent Persian physician was the scholar known as Avicenna, who is sometimes called the Arab Aristotle. A native of Bukhara in present-day Turkistan, his full name was Abu Ali al-Husayn ibn Abd Allah ibn Sina. He was a gifted student who mastered the science of medicine while still a youth. By the time he was eighteen years old, Avicenna also knew algebra, was thoroughly versed in Greek and Persian philosophy, and could recite the Koran. Later in life, he would compile an encyclopedia of all the knowledge current in the Middle East of his day.

Avicenna's best-known works were medical writings. Like most of his contemporaries, he believed that the destiny of every human being was written in the stars, including matters pertaining to health. He drew a mental link between each part of the body and one of the planets, and he timed his treatments accordingly. Avicenna also reaffirmed the old Greek idea of correspondence between the planets and the various metals.

Heavenly configurations thus became vitally important in his approach to the Hermetic arts. Oddly enough, however, he seemed to blow hot and cold on alchemy at different points in his career. "As to the claims of the alchemists," he once flatly declared, "it must be clearly understood that it is not in their power to bring about any change of metallic species." But he went on to admit that "they can make excellent imitations." From Avicenna's other writings it is clear that he devoted many years to the pursuit of the philosophers' stone.

For all his learning and lasting renown, Avicenna did not fare especially well in his lifetime. For a while he served as grand vizier at Bukhara and then, when the local government collapsed, he moved to a court position at Hamadan in western Persia. But he developed a fatal taste for high living, in particular for women and wine. When Avicenna's behavior became a court scandal, he was stripped of his posts and finally died in obscurity at Hamadan in 1037. He was only fifty-six years old.

During the years of Arab ascendancy, Europe was mired in the cultural decline known as the Dark Ages. When the Continent began to recover its bearings during the eleventh century, it turned in part to the texts of the great Arabic scholars for inspiration and authority. This led to the rediscovery of the ancient Greek philosophers and scientists. And soon monks and friars were scribbling away, transcribing into Latin the thoughts of Plato and Aristotle, Pythagoras, and Democritus, along with the manuscripts of Geber, Rhasis, and Avicenna.

The flow of ideas from the Middle East to Europe was somewhat surprising, since generations of bloodshed had divided Islam from Christendom, and the conflict was still raging. Between wars, however, scholars from the opposing camps would meet and converse, particularly in the border regions of southern France and Moorish Spain. And almost inevitably, the topics included alchemy.

Among the leading centers of cultural exchange was the University of Montpellier, near the foothills of the French Pyrenees. Along with a handful of lawyers and physicians, the majority of the students at this institution were men of the Church. The curriculum revolved around medicine, Latin, Greek, and Arabic. But Montpellier was also the crucible of European alchemy, and a great many of the early medieval adepts seem to have studied there.

Two of the more influential members of the Montpellier community were Albertus Magnus, the most brilliant scholar of his generation, and Thomas Aquinas, his star pupil. Both men were Dominican monks and deeply religious, but the two were also eager devotees of the teachings of Aristotle. The clear, cool analysis of the Greek philosopher did not blend easily with the demands of Christian faith, so both erudite clerics took it upon themselves to reconcile the contradictions between the two views.

As a youth in the early years of the thirteenth century,

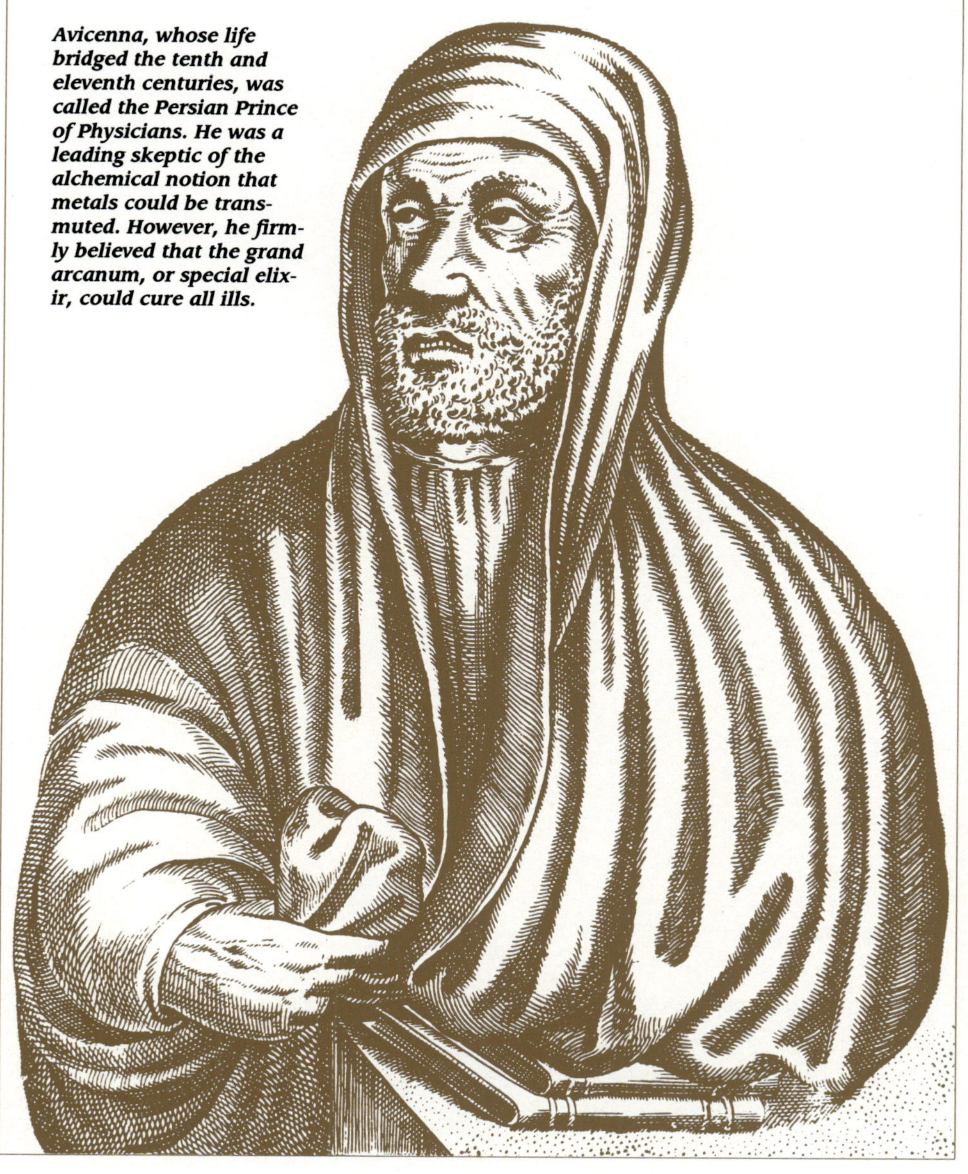

Avicenna, whose life bridged the tenth and eleventh centuries, was called the Persian Prince of Physicians. He was a leading skeptic of the alchemical notion that metals could be transmuted. However, he firmly believed that the grand arcanum, or special elixir, could cure all ills.

Albertus had hardly seemed destined for the role of scholar. He was the son of a noble family from Swabia in Germany and, if anything, had impressed his elders as a hopelessly backward child. Later in life he would claim that the Virgin Mary had granted him the gift of high intelligence in a personal visitation. Whether or not this was the case, he would hold professorships in Paris and Cologne at two of the great European universities and would serve a stint as bishop of Regensburg. At the height of his fame, he was widely referred to as the Universal Doctor, the wisest man of the century.

"Were there enough mercury," thirteenth-century Spanish alchemist Ramon Llull (right) is reported to have said, "I could transform whole oceans into gold." A mystic with a missionary bent, Llull by one account was stoned to death in Tunis in 1315, while he was attempting to convert Muslims to Christianity.

By inclination, Albertus was a scientist first and foremost, and he delighted in observing nature. No thinker of his time did more to promote the logical approach of Aristotelian science in medieval Europe. Albertus was one of a scattering of scientists who took the trouble to dissect animals to further his understanding of anatomy. He also wrote a groundbreaking treatise on botany and was a skilled tinkerer, inventing a new kind of pistol. On top of all this, Albertus spent long hours in his laboratory mixing the potions that figured in alchemical lore.

It is worth noting, however, that Albertus never claimed to be an alchemist himself. Indeed, he cautioned against "deceivers" who said they were creating gold when in fact they were really only coloring inferior metals with a gold tint. Nevertheless, he was obviously fascinated by alchemy and wrote extensively on the subject. He discussed, among other things, a current theory that metals could be "cured" of their impurities by sprinkling them with an elixir—much the way symptoms of physical illness were relieved by administering a tonic. To Albertus, there seemed to be no obvious reason why sulfur and mercury could not be blended together to make gold, provided all the ingredients had been sufficiently refined in advance.

Although Dominican priest Albertus Magnus was skeptical about alchemical beliefs, legend said he possessed the philosophers' stone, and that his pupil Thomas Aquinas destroyed it.

So great was the prestige of Albertus Magnus that he became the subject of many fanciful tales. Perhaps the most peculiar of these was the legend of Albertus's robot. In his study—or at least, so the story goes—he kept a bronze statue that had been cast by his pupil Thomas Aquinas. One day, Albertus anointed the figurine with an elixir, causing it to spring to life. For a time, the statue proved extremely useful, for it willingly ran errands, swept the floor, and performed various other domestic chores. The robot had a major drawback, however: It had a tendency to chatter incessantly. The noise eventually proved so disruptive that Aquinas took a hammer and pounded the robot to scrap.

Among the Christians of the thirteenth century, the creation of life was generally regarded as the exclusive right of the Almighty. It is possible, therefore, that the dubious story of Albertus's robot helper was circulated to bring to light the ethical considerations surrounding the work of the alchemists. The scholar's protégé, Thomas Aquinas, agonized over such issues and all matters of conflict between reason and faith. In his lifelong effort to resolve the contradictions between the teachings of the Church and those of the Greek philosophers, he developed many of the fundamental principles of Roman Catholic theology. Aquinas rejected alchemy, believing that its power was derived from the devil rather than from nature. But even he stopped short of denying the virtues of alchemical elixirs and the philosophers' stone.

The scruples of Saint Thomas did little to dampen his contemporaries' enthusiasm. Arnau de Villanova, a Spanish physician who taught at the University of Montpellier, was said to have acquired such formidable magical powers that he was able to create a living human being by incubating chemicals inside a pumpkin. Arnau was a firm believer in the philosophers' stone, which he claimed could cure in a single day maladies that otherwise would last a month. He also believed the stone could make gold and was rumored to have used it for that purpose.

Arnau's colleague, the Franciscan friar Ramon Llull, apparently believed that the stone could give life to plants "by its great and marvelous heat." He suggested that a grain of the miraculous substance, dissolved in water and sprinkled over a grape vine, would cause the vine to bear ripe fruit by the month of May. Llull would eventually become famous as a scholar of Arabic and as a missionary, but he was a bit of a rake as a young man. According to one account, he was rash enough to gallop on horseback into the cathedral at Majorca to impress a young lady. Like Albertus Magnus before him, however, he was visited by what he claimed to be a beatific vision, in his case at the age of thirty. From that time forward, he devoted himself to the Church, risking his life in the dangerous task of bringing Christianity to the Moors of North Africa. Llull also wrote extensively on science and theology, using a cryptic notation of his own devising. Perhaps it was this use of code that earned him a reputation as an alchemist.

In any event, the story survives that he once journeyed to London and there enriched the coffers of King Edward II by transmuting 50,000 pounds of lead, tin, and mercury into gold. The fact that no record exists showing that Llull ever crossed the English Channel has never seemed to bother the mystic's admirers.

England grew alchemists of its own, in any case. The greatest by far was Roger Bacon, a Franciscan friar and Ox-

Thirteenth-century Englishman Roger Bacon, perhaps the most important alchemist of his era, tried repeatedly to make gold but never succeeded. "Nature alwaies intendeth and striveth to the perfection of Gold," he insisted, "but many accidents come between."

ford don of extraordinary learning and achievement. All sorts of fantastic tales have been told about Bacon: He was accused of having conjured the elements, of summoning the devil, of fabricating a mirror that revealed the future, and of sculpting a brass head capable of talking. His true contribution to the world was far more important: In the acquisition of knowledge, Bacon made a sharp distinction between logic and experience, between so-called truths discovered in libraries and those derived from firsthand observation. Other scholars had suggested this idea—Geber, for one—but no one pursued it as rigorously as Bacon. His approach to learning became the cornerstone of the scientific method—the modern practice of scientific inquiry.

"Through experiment," wrote Bacon, the scholar "gains knowledge of the things pertaining to nature and medicine and alchemy, and all that is in heaven and in the earth beneath." Of these, alchemy held a position of primary importance. Bacon believed wholeheartedly in transmutation, and his observations seemed to confirm it. An iron pot placed in copper sulfate did indeed appear to change to copper. The purest water, left to evaporate in a glass container, deposited a distinct residue, apparently having transformed itself into earth.

The creation of gold proved more elusive. Bacon accepted the mercury-sulfur theory, but he never managed to make the process work. Nonetheless, he believed that the work of the alchemist—successful or not—was worthy in its own right. He compared the pursuit of transmutation to a man hunting treasure in his garden: Even if the seeker never found the prize, he had at very least cultivated the soil and thereby increased his harvest. "So the search and endeavors to make gold have brought many useful inventions and instructive experiments to light."

One of Bacon's contributions that stemmed from his experiments with alchemy was a method for purifying saltpeter, which is an important component of gunpowder. He also made significant strides in optics, grinding a magnifying glass that could ignite a candle with the concentrated rays of even a dim light source. And there is some reason to believe that he devised a primitive telescope.

Like many adepts of the period, Bacon found himself continually in hot water with the ecclesiastical authorities. His philosophy of embracing the dictates of logic and scientific observation was threatening to his Franciscan superiors, and they persuaded Pope Urban IV to place him under house arrest. In 1284, he was jailed by Pope Nicholas IV, and he would remain in prison for the next ten years. Bacon died not long after his release; he was about eighty years old. According to one report of his death, he was the victim of a laboratory explosion.

Bacon's Spanish contemporaries fared little better. Ramon Llull's odd encrypted manuscripts aroused suspicion and brought charges of heresy. Shrugging off his critics, he returned to North Africa to preach the Gospel. But the Moors had no patience for infidels, and after repeated imprisonments, Llull was eventually stoned to death. Arnau de Villanova died in a shipwreck at the age of seventy-five, but not before he had been harassed by the Inquisition for his supposed heresy and witchcraft. His writings were banned by the pope.

A pattern had been set that would be played out for years to come. Along with the likes of Roger Bacon, the greatest and most provocative alchemists assumed an oddly contradictory role in their societies. They would be the archivists and lovers of tradition, reaching back for an esoteric wisdom presumed to be lost. At the same time they became the futurists, dauntlessly rattling the gates of scientific understanding. And their lives would never be simple. In 1317, for instance, John XXII issued a papal bull denouncing alchemy, and the external pressures on those involved in what came to be called the great work became increasingly severe. Nonetheless, as time passed, popular interest in the alchemists' work increased. More and more rich and powerful individuals—hoping to be rewarded with untold wealth or even immortality—demonstrated an eagerness to sponsor their experiments. When the Renaissance flooded Europe with intellectual light in the fifteenth century, it also brought the dawn of alchemy's golden age.

A Visit to the Laboratory

The typical alchemist's laboratory in Renaissance Europe was a dark, cluttered place that stank of smoke and mysterious chemicals. Many alchemists worked at home, in order to save money and avoid outside interference. Some settled in the kitchen, to take advantage of the cooking fire. Others chose the attic or cellar, where late-night activity was less likely to be noticed by inquisitive neighbors.

These small, makeshift laboratories were often filled with a grimy jumble of instruments, manuscripts, skulls, animal specimens, and assorted mystical objects. Most alchemists also found room for an altar—an aid they deemed essential to the spiritual aspects of their pursuit.

In these surroundings that owed more to mysticism than to science, adepts searching for the philosophers' stone inadvertently laid much of the groundwork for the later discipline of applied chemistry. Alchemists were the first to isolate a number of chemicals, from phosphorus to hydrochloric acid, and they also developed new equipment and methods for distilling fluids, assaying metals, and controlling chemical reactions. Some of their devices and techniques are presented in the photographs and paintings on the following pages.

Tending the Alchemical Fire

"A perfect Master ye may call him true, that knoweth his Heates both high and lowe," wrote Thomas Norton, a fifteenth-century British alchemist. Heat was the fundamental requirement of nearly every alchemical process, from distilling dew to smelting lead. To achieve and maintain just the right temperature, alchemists experimented with a number of furnaces, water baths, and other heating apparatus. The self-regulating furnace below stayed hot without tending: Once started with bellows, its charcoal fire supplied itself with air by an ingenious draft system.

Given an alchemist's limited funds, however, furnaces could be as crude as the household fire vigorously tended by a rural experimenter in Adriaen van Ostade's *Alchemist (right),* painted in 1667. In this homey scene, with busy wife and snacking child in the dimly lit background, the alchemical craft is reduced to its essentials—a single book, a pair of spectacles perched on a stool, a few distilling vessels, and the all-important fire.

The Delicate Process of Distillation

To obtain purified substances, alchemists often resorted to distillation. Because Arabian alchemists had refined the process, Europeans used Arabic names for most distilling vessels. For example, the alembic *(below, right)*—a flask in which vapor rising from the heated liquid in the bottom section condensed in the cooler dome at the top and then was channeled into a long spout—took its name from *al-anbiq,* the Arab term for a still.

An exception to that nomenclature was the two-armed "pelican" *(below, left)*. In this device, vapor condensed against the glass walls of the upper chamber, then trickled back down to the lower chamber to be redistilled. Possibly because it resembled a bird pecking its chest, the vessel was named for the creature that, in medieval belief, nourished its young with blood drawn from its own breast.

Distilling vessels abound in *The Alchemist and His Workshop (left),* a seventeenth-century painting by Thomas Wyck that portrays the workroom of a successful adept, seen at left in a black cap. As the master contemplates his books, assistants tend distilling furnaces, each capped with a classic alembic.

Mixing and Measuring Key Materials

The ultimate goal of the alchemist's labors was "projection," the transmutation of a base metal. Although the task would seem nonsensical to a modern chemist, projection involved several tools that later proved useful in scientific laboratories.

Mortar and pestle *(below, right),* for instance, were intended to be employed by alchemists to grind pieces of the philosophers' stone, and other materials, into dust. Powdered ingredients could then be combined with metals in a crucible *(below, center),* a small pot with a cross-shaped rim of four spouts to allow easy pouring. In David Ryckaert's *Alchemist's Workshop (left),* a crucible heating in the fireplace is one of several vessels in use by a scholar whose meditative expression suggests alchemy's mystical side.

Unlike later scientists, alchemists rarely measured exact quantities, but they did hope to weigh the gold resulting from projection. Such was the supreme, if perhaps never fulfilled, purpose of the alchemical scales below, ancestor of today's laboratory balance.

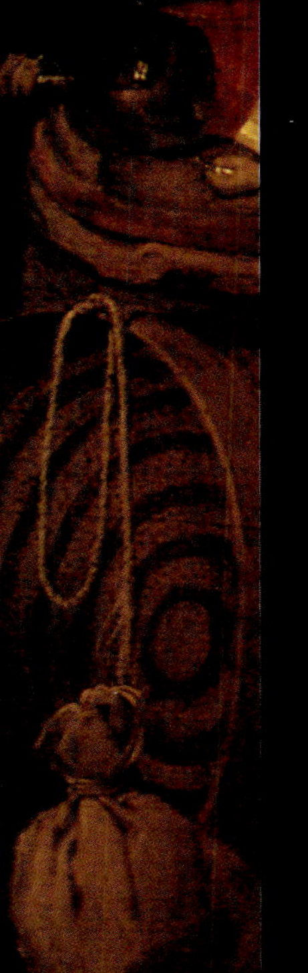

CHAPTER 2

Alchemy's Golden Age

Strolling the grounds of a small mosque in the town of Broussa, in what is now Turkey, a seventeenth-century French traveler named Paul Lucas had a strange encounter. He was introduced to a dervish, a monk in a mystic Muslim sect. Although Lucas had experienced many adventures during his journey through Greece and the Middle East, nothing prepared him for what he was to hear from his new acquaintance.

"He was a man in every way extraordinary in learning," Lucas wrote admiringly after a long conversation with the dervish, "and in external appearance he seemed to be about thirty years old, but from his discourse I was persuaded he had lived a century." At first their talk centered on religion and philosophy. But gradually the subject turned to alchemy, or the "sublime science," as the dervish called it, and more specifically to the quest for the philosophers' stone and the stone's supposed power to confer immortality—or in the monk's view, near immortality. He avowed that all people eventually die, but that any master of alchemy who possessed the stone, "by the use of the true medicine, can ward off whatever may hinder or impair the animal functions for a thousand years."

Lucas responded loftily that most Frenchmen of sense considered the philosophers' stone to be a fiction. As proof, Lucas proposed the name of Nicholas Flamel, one of France's most renowned alchemists and one who reportedly had possessed the stone. Flamel had lived in Paris during the latter half of the fourteenth century. He had amassed great wealth and had earned a saintly and enduring reputation by spending most of his fortune on charitable works. Nonetheless, Lucas pointed out smugly, Flamel had died in 1417, stone or no stone, after a lengthy but decidedly mortal existence of eighty-seven years.

The dervish "smiled at my simplicity," Lucas wrote, "and asked with an air of mirth: 'Do you really believe this? No, no, my friend, Flamel is still living; neither he nor his wife are dead!' " Then, before the startled Lucas could say a word, the mystic silenced him utterly. "It is not above three years since I left both the one and the other in the Indies," he said. "He is one of my best friends."

By then, if the dervish spoke the truth, Flamel would have been well over 300 years old, and his lifetime would have encompassed the era of alchemy's greatest flourishing. The fact is that by the end of the seventeenth century, popular acceptance of the "sublime science" was so widespread that many believers would not have been in the least surprised by the dervish's startling news. Indeed, reports of Flamel's extraordinary longevity would continue to surface for at least another century.

This era, the Renaissance, was alchemy's golden age. The wave of rebirth and renewal washing over Europe brought dazzling innovations to all the arts and sciences. Religion, too, experienced mighty changes with the Protestant Reformation that began early in the sixteenth century. Alchemy—part science, part art, part religion—rode buoyantly on the swell of innovation, particularly as it applied to the eternal human pursuit of gold.

Gold truly symbolized the alchemist's quest, and kings and commoners from the Mediterranean to the Baltic came to see alchemy as a shortcut to inexhaustible wealth. Because greed spawns corruption, there was a darker side to all this. Europe abounded with charlatans, swindlers, and humbugs who preyed on the humble and the powerful alike. Their histories provide a rich catalog of the weaknesses as well as the follies of humankind.

Yet in its true form the art of arts was a high calling, and many alchemists were men of great wisdom and profound moral purpose. For them the search for spiritual perfection took precedence over the quest for easy riches, and transforming a leaden and impure soul into spiritual gold was as important as the physical process of transmuting metals. These genuine adepts saw the universe as a unity and believed that by exploring the intricate workings of its parts they could divine the meaning of the whole.

Thus they viewed their lofty vocation as a holy art that contained a dual nature. Diligently pursued, it could provide both a spiritual path to knowledge of the cosmic purpose and a practical means to improve the lot of humankind. As the yeasty spirit of the Renaissance inspired thinkers to question ancient authority and seek functional answers to nature's mysteries, alchemists were in the front lines of the new order. They paved the way for the development of chemistry as a science. And since true alchemists had selected as one of their goals the betterment of the human condition, it was a logical next step for them to apply their chemical skills to the field of medicine.

To achieve such enlightenment was a formidable undertaking, however, and the difficult path led a large number of alchemists to a lifetime of disappointment and a pauper's grave. Yet on its highest plane alchemy was a magnificent obsession, and the true adept had

nothing but scorn for the petty practitioner whose only goal in life consisted of a base desire to find his fortune in a gold-filled crucible.

When Nicholas Flamel was making a name for himself in fourteenth-century Paris, the dawn of the age of scientific chemistry was a long way off. Flamel and his fellow alchemists knew almost nothing about the structure of matter. Most scholars believed firmly in the ancient theory that all matter sprang from an elemental material, known as the *prima materia,* from which was formed the four basic elements—fire, air, water, and earth. They still embraced Aristotle's explanation that everything in the universe was fashioned from these four elements and that the precise proportions, combined with contrasting qualities such as wet and dry, hot and cold, determined whether a metal, say, turned out to be lead or gold.

In this context, the idea of transmutation made perfect sense. The metals themselves, most scholars thought, were naturally fashioned in the earth's interior furnace by an essentially alchemical process that acted on the prima materia. Furthermore, since all things in nature were charged with the divine spirit and therefore aspired to a higher, more perfect state, metals, too, gradually perfected themselves in the earth's womb. Thus even lead, through a natural process of transmutation, would eventually turn into silver or gold. The alchemist's task, therefore, was to speed up nature's work by performing the transmutation in the laboratory. Such artificial transmutation seemed entirely reasonable to Renaissance thinkers. The problem was how to go about it.

One vital part of the answer was the mysterious agent known as the philosophers' stone, described by the fourth-century alchemist Zosimus as a "stone which is not a stone." This substance, which carried literally hundreds of other names—such as the "powder of projection," the "virgin's milk," and the "shade of the sun"—was credited with miraculous powers. Not only could it help transmute base metals into gold, it reputedly could soften glass, render its owner invisible at will, or give an alchemist the ability to levitate. A few people believed that the stone would enable them to converse with angels or even to understand the language of animals.

Closely related to the stone, and often synonymous

with it, was the elixir of life, whose specific attribute was the power to cure disease and stave off death. It was this aspect of the stone that gradually came to command more attention among alchemists and laymen alike during the sixteenth century, as the practice of medicine inched toward a more scientific approach.

As for making gold, the elusive stone was considered an indispensable ingredient in the transmutation process. Usually in the form of a red powder, the stone was venerated as the vital catalyst in elaborate recipes for making gold. Thus, the alchemist's first and greatest labor was to create the stone. Everything else was thought to be easy. Making the stone was not.

All agreed that the starting point was the prima materia, although few had a firm notion of what that meant. So the initial step in creating the stone involved the search for the prima materia. Generations of alchemists spent lifetimes poring over ancient manuscripts in hopes of finding the secret hidden among the intricate symbolism of earlier adepts. They also toiled unceasingly in their laboratories to find the precious formula through experimentation, a labor that was generally known as the "great work." There were as many theories about how to pursue the great work as there were alchemists, and each one carefully guarded his theories, experiments, and even the apparatus used in the process.

One of the basic tenets of alchemy was that its secrets must not be revealed to the uninitiated. "I swear to you upon my soul," the thirteenth-century alchemist Ramon Llull vowed to his readers, "that if you reveal this, you shall be damned." A later adept, writing under the name of Basil Valentine, was no less explicit when he warned that "to speak of this even a little further would mean being willing to sink into hell."

One of the few relics of supposedly immortal alchemist Nicholas Flamel (far left) is this conventional medieval tombstone, the back of which was being employed as a grocer's cutting board when the stone was rediscovered more than a hundred years ago. Those who believe that Flamel did achieve eternal life consider the tombstone to be part of an elaborate ruse that was used to conceal his accomplishment.

The reasons for secrecy went beyond mere elitism. Greed, of course, played its part in prompting some alchemists to keep their formulas under wraps. Another powerful restraint was imposed when the Catholic church in the fourteenth century pronounced alchemy to be a diabolic art. But still more compelling, for the true adept, was a genuine fear of the evil that might be wreaked on society should the stone find its way into the wrong hands. As Englishman Thomas Norton wrote in the fifteenth century: "This art must ever secret be. / The cause whereof is this, as ye may see: / If one evil man had thereof all his will, / All Christian peace he might easily spill, / And with his pride he might pull down / Rightful kings and princes of renown."

Norton's apprehension may sound quaint today, but he was in dead earnest, and it would not be outlandish to liken his concern to a twentieth-century statesman's anxiety about nuclear proliferation.

The stone may not have been part of the Renaissance citizens' everyday life, but most of them believed that it existed and that some of the sorcerers, necromancers, and wizards floating about possessed it. Written and oral histories of the period abound with tales of the stone's prowess, and the narratives (some might call them legends or fairy tales) deal in perfectly matter-of-fact tones with the phenomenon. Most of the accounts appear today to be an intriguing blend of truth and wishful thinking, but not all the facts can be sorted out, and many mysteries remain.

Nicholas Flamel's story, a compound of his own writings, municipal records, and anecdotes, was one of the best-known tales of the stone during the Renaissance, particularly in France. With a compulsion that seems to have been fundamental to the alchemist's makeup, Flamel spent most of his life seeking the stone. When he found it, the story goes, he not only did well by society but was himself rewarded with earthly wealth, spiritual refinement, and a place among the immortals.

Flamel was born around 1330 of poor parents, but he got enough education to achieve the respected role of public scrivener. He operated out of two tiny shops in Paris, where he spent his days hunched over a desk reproducing manuscripts. By all accounts, his work earned him a modest living, and marriage brought him both an attractive wife and a sizable dowry. That much seems believable enough; it is the rest of the story that requires a leap of faith. One night Flamel is said to have dreamed that he saw a book in the hands of an angel. "Flamel," commanded the angel, "behold this book of which thou understandest nothing; to many others but thyself it would remain forever unintelligible, but one day thou shalt discern in its pages what none but thyself will see."

The book itself was extraordinary: Bound in finely wrought copper, the leaves were made not of paper or parchment but of thin bark. Across the first leaf ran an inscription in gold dedicating the book to the Jewish people and signed by "Abraham the Jew, prince, priest, astrologer and philosopher." Intrigued, Flamel reached out for the book, only to see it and the angel vanish in a flash of light. The alchemist awoke empty handed and puzzled by the vision, which he would describe much later as a revelation.

According to the story, the next development occurred some years afterward, in 1357. While browsing through a number of old manuscripts, Flamel stumbled upon the very volume he had seen in his dream. He bought the book on the spot for the minuscule sum of two florins. Returning home, he pored over his purchase and easily read the "good and intelligible Latin" text. But that ease was deceptive, for although the text was obviously a guide to transmuting metals, it assumed that the reader had an understanding of the secret Jewish mystical doctrine called the Cabala as well as a command of alchemy. And by some accounts it assumed, moreover, that the reader already possessed the philosophers' stone. Even more bewildering were the highly symbolic illuminations that appeared throughout the volume. Flamel could only hope that somewhere in these exquisitely rendered drawings of winged gods and writhing dragons, of slain infants and flowering rose trees, lay the key that would unlock the text and reveal the identity of the prima materia as well as the process that would transform it into the philosophers' stone.

Flamel worked diligently to solve the book's mysteries. He confided in his wife, Pernelle, and eventually sought the counsel of some of Paris's most learned men. But no one could help him understand. "I went through a thousand labyrinths or processes," wrote Flamel of those frustrating years, "but all in vain."

One problem was that he could find no Jewish scholar to help him decipher the tome. Anti-Semitic persecution had hounded most French Jews from the country. Many of them had settled in Spain. By now obsessed with his quest, Flamel decided to travel to Spain in search of a rabbi to consult about the manuscript. Dressed as a pilgrim, with a copy of part of the text sewn into his clothing for security, he joined other supplicants making the arduous trek across the Pyrenees to the famous shrine of Santiago de Compostela at the western rim of Spain. Only after reaching the distant shrine and returning partway home, disappointed and weary, did he finally find the man he sought.

At an inn in the city of León he met a rabbi by the name of Master Canches, who took one look at the excerpt from the book of Abraham the Jew and reacted, in Flamel's own words, "with great astonishment and joy." Canches immediately began to decipher the excerpt, and soon a delighted Flamel was making plans to return to France, with the rabbi in tow, so that they could take on the entire text. But the two got only as far as Orléans, declared Flamel, when Canches fell violently ill with a fever. A week later, the rabbi was dead.

Flamel returned to Paris alone, but thanks to Canches, he now knew the identity of the prima materia, although the process that would convert it into the philosophers' stone remained a mystery. By Flamel's account, he redoubled his efforts to solve the puzzle, an endeavor that he later described as the "thing most difficult above all other things in the world"—words that echoed the experience of hundreds of other alchemists through the centuries.

Three years later, though, on January 17, 1382, Flamel finally claimed success. He reported that with the faithful Pernelle at his side, he transmuted a half-pound of mercury into silver "finer than the silver which is mined." Three months later, bursting with excitement, he attempted a second experiment and this time is alleged to have succeeded in producing pure gold.

Flamel supposedly performed only one more transmutation. Nevertheless, this unassuming scribe, whose life had been comfortable but by no means extravagant, suddenly became the wealthy benefactor of a number of religious and charitable institutions. According to contemporary records, he and Pernelle would found and endow fourteen hospitals, three chapels, and seven churches in Paris alone, and a like number in Boulogne.

Flamel's benefactions are chronicled in reputable municipal records. But whether his largess was the happy result of alchemy, as he claimed, or merely the consequence of a lifetime of penny-pinching has been the subject of speculation ever since.

For all his supposed prosperity, Flamel appears to have died as modestly as he lived. In his will, he left little behind: another bequest to charity, a bequest to the chambermaid (she apparently took the place in his affections of the beloved Pernelle, who by this account had died some years before he did), and a small remainder of cash. A burial service was held for him in 1418 at the church of Saint Jacques-la-Boucherie. Chiseled on the tombstone was an epitaph that he wrote himself: "From earth I have come, to earth I return."

Less convincing than these factual details, but still tantalizing, are the stories of Flamel's supposed miraculous survival. According to the wise old dervish whom Paul Lucas interviewed, neither Flamel nor Pernelle died when they were thought to have done so. Faking their own deaths, and substituting blocks of wood to simulate corpses in their coffins, husband and wife slipped off to Switzerland and with the help of the philosophers' stone lived on for centuries, enjoying, as Lucas reported, "a philosophic life, sometimes in one country, sometimes in another."

Lucas's was not the only account of Flamel's survival. Decades later, in the eighteenth century, an aged cleric, one Sire Marcel, reported seeing Flamel working in an underground laboratory in the heart of Paris, sequestered behind seven closed doors. Once again, in 1761, the peripatetic Flamel and Pernelle were supposedly sighted in the audience at the Paris Opera. Not only that, it was seriously reported that the couple—both would have been in their mid-four hundreds by then—were accompanied by a son, who, it was said, had been born to them in India. Finally, as late as 1818, a man claiming to be Nicholas Flamel made the rounds of Paris coffeehouses offering to disclose his secrets to any and all comers willing to part with the enormous sum of 300,000 francs.

This greedy, latter-day incarnation of Nicholas Flamel would seem to have little in common with the quiet, scholarly scribe whose deep religious faith was never doubted and who used his wealth, whatever its source, to do good works for the poor. So pious was Flamel, in fact, that he published his own prayers. Freely acknowledging the hand of God as his partner in the great work, he never failed to thank "the Lord God of my life" who "hast given into my possession the fountains and well-springs of all the treasures and riches of this world."

Flamel's reported successes were at least partly responsible for the growing interest in alchemy in the fifteenth century and, to a lesser extent, for an increasing perception of alchemy as a spiritual pursuit rather than simply as a means to riches. He was followed by a host of high-minded adepts for whom the true aim of the great work was the spiritual transformation of the alchemist himself. Prominent among such "chemical philosophers" was an English monk who was born around 1415, just about the time when—officially at least—Nicholas Flamel died. The monk's name was George Ripley, and like Flamel he would give credit to God, "the granter of such secret ways," as the unseen force in his laboratory. He, too, spent many years puz-

An Enigmatic Guide to the Secret Art

Eighteen feet long when fully unrolled, the medieval Ripley scroll presented here and on the following pages offers a seemingly endless series of alchemical enigmas. Attributed to fifteenth-century English monk George Ripley, the scroll is thought to describe the so-called black, white, and red stages of the alchemist's work, but any and all further details remain open to interpretation. Despite this mystery, or perhaps because of it, the scroll was so popular that at least twenty illuminated copies are known.

Under a Latin inscription that begins, "The mysterious stone is shrouded in a secret source," a bearded and cowled alchemist broods over a flask that contains a toad. The inscription on the arms of the vessel exhorts him to "make water of earth, and earth of air, and air of fire, and fire of earth," a reference to the complex process of transmutation that lies ahead.

Within the flask, encircled allegorical scenes radiate from a closed book inspected by a king and a monk. The scene at upper right labeled prima materia may represent the alchemist's raw material; the other circles are thought to signify the seven alchemical metals. Under the flask, references to "Black Sea" and "Black Solle" may identify this as the first, or black, stage of the great work.

Beneath a fire heating the alchemist's vessel is a quotation from a thirteenth-century adept, Arnau de Villanova, describing his vision of an old man bearing a book with binding clasps of silver and pages of gold. Some think this passage inspired the Ripley scroll.

A ten-leaved tree of life begins the next section of the scroll. On the tree, a dragon-woman and a radiant youth bear the Latin words for spirit and soul, concepts that are also symbolized by feathers that shower from the nearby sun and moon.

In another mysterious scene, seven alchemists man the turrets of a castle that encloses a mystical pool. Emerging from the water, a couple some identify as Adam and Eve eat grapes from vines clinging to the tree above. On the wall of the castle, the phrases "White Sea" and "White Lune" suggest this is the second, or white, stage of the alchemical process.

Surrounded by another body of water that may represent the red, or final, stage of alchemy, a giant accompanied by two celestial figures supports the pedestal of the castle above. Vessels at the pool's four corners contain the Aristotelian elements of fire, water, air, and earth. Below the pool, a green dragon spits out a toad.

Above an inscription marking the final steps of the red stage, two lions face each other across a burning door. The poem below offers enigmatic guidance under a cautionary heading: "Beware and hereof be wise."

Drenched by rain or dew from above, an eagle with the head of a king perches on a sphere that some consider a symbol of both the world and the alchemical vessel. Identified below as the Bird of Hermes, this creature may represent Ripley's phantasmagorical vision of the philosophers' stone—a phoenix created out of fire to bring the world to golden perfection.

Beneath a banner marking the creation of the red elixir of life, or philosophers' stone, is a sun containing three interlocked spheres that resemble a modern diagram of a molecular structure. The poem alongside the crescent moon praises both sun and moon for their influences, without which the stone could not have been produced.

A dragon cryptically identified as the Serpent of Arabia bites both the moon and its own tail as it drips blood from a deep abdominal wound. Dragon's blood was a common alchemical symbol for the highly corrosive aqua fortis, or nitric acid.

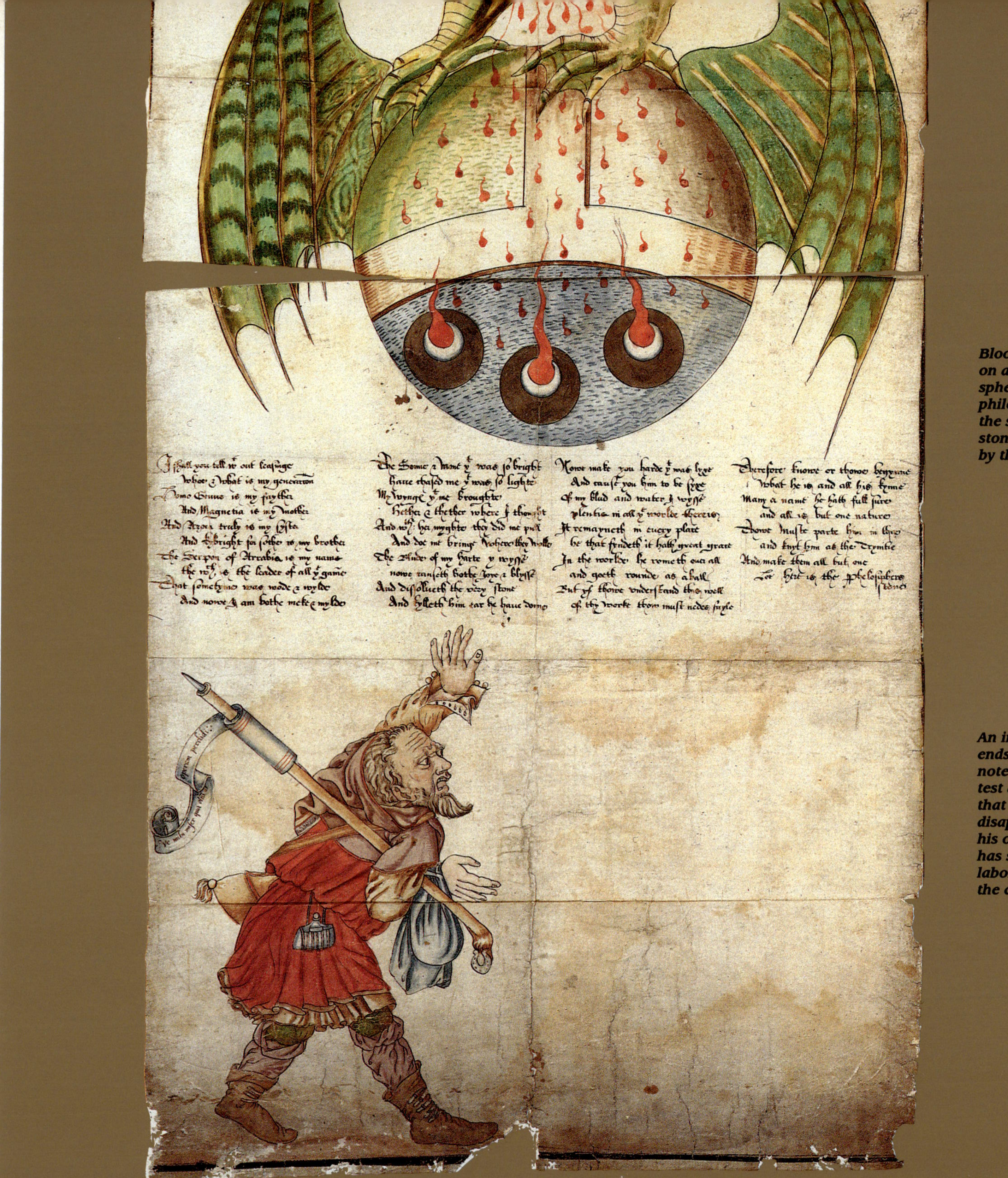

Blood from the wounded dragon above falls onto a winged sphere that may represent the philosophers' stone. Beneath the sphere, a poem explains the stone can be dissolved only by the blood of a dragon.

An impoverished alchemist ends the scroll on an ironic note. Raising his hand in protest at the fruitless pursuits that have consumed his life, the disappointed laborer shoulders his own scroll: "Pity me who has squandered my oil and labor." By oil, he may mean the costly fuel used in his lab.

zling over books before journeying to distant places in search of the secret of the philosophers' stone. Somewhere along the way, legend says, he found it, for when he eventually reached the island of Rhodes, he is said to have created a fortune in gold, which he donated to the Knights of Saint John of Jerusalem.

Returning to England, Ripley devoted the remainder of his long life to the mastery of what his renowned student Philalethes called the "divine skill." Before his death in 1490, the Englishman managed to fill twenty-four books with all he had learned.

But Ripley's works, replete with rich imagery and confusing symbolism, did little to make the practice of alchemy any more understandable. His poem "The Vision of Sir George Ripley," for example, tells of a toad that gorged itself on grape juice until it finally burst. The toad was left to putrefy for "Eighty days and Four," before being roasted over a "gentle Fire" until it oozed a venom. Scholarly analysis of the poem reveals it as an opaque recipe for transforming gold (the toad), via the processes of alchemy, into a tincture that supposedly could be used to cure all diseases.

In *The Compound of Alchemie,* written in 1471, Ripley spells out the twelve steps involved in his version of the great work. These steps resemble the twelve gates of a "philosopher's castle," each one leading to the next, until at last, as Ripley promises his readers, "all the Castell thou holdyst at wyll."

The entire process, beginning with calcination (burning a substance to an ash or powder) and ending with projection (creating gold), could take a year or longer, since the first steps involved reducing a base metal to prima materia. After repeated vaporization and condensation, a step called exaltation would produce a red powder. This was the philosophers' stone, which could then be added to any base metal and heated in a crucible until the metal was transformed into gold.

For Ripley, though, this was not the real point of the exercise. What was more important to him was his comparison of the twelve chemical steps to a kind of spiritual obstacle course. In this concept, the first hurdle, calcination, corresponds to the self-reproach that sears away the husk of human shortcomings to reveal the inner person. In subsequent steps, that inner person is separated into spirit, soul, and body before undergoing a mock death and spiritual rebirth that culminates in the reunion of a purified spirit and a purified body.

Admittedly, for every high-principled adept like Ripley, the golden age of alchemy produced many more practitioners whose approach to the art was simply an unbridled rush to produce gold in the laboratory. The undisciplined fondness of these alchemists for the furnace and the bellows earned them the nickname of "puffers" and the scorn of the more philosophically inclined adepts. As one adept wrote: "False alchemists seek only to make gold; true philosophers desire only knowledge. The former produce mere tinctures, sophistries, ineptitudes; the latter enquire after the principles of things." The puffers' efforts may not have produced their cherished dreams of wealth, but they did not all toil in vain. Their work eventually led to the discovery of previously unknown elements and to new knowledge about the behavior of various chemical compounds.

Sometimes a puffer's experiments ended in tragedy, especially if he had the misfortune to set off an explosion or to inhale too many noxious fumes. Such was the lot of one bellows blower, who, according to a sixteenth-century account, hid himself away in his laboratory in a vain effort to concoct gold for his wealthy patroness. For two years he toiled and for two years she paid the bills for great quantities of lead and charcoal that went up in smoke. Finally, she demanded to see the laboratory and got a glimpse of hell itself, with the soot-covered alchemist hovering over "enormous cauldrons, long tubes, furnaces, and three or four scorching fires blazing in various parts of what felt like the interior of a volcano." Promising to apply himself even more diligently than he had before, the miserable puffer came to a bad end when a thundering explosion instantly transmuted the laboratory,

Under their master's watchful eye, men armed with ropes, a weight, and a knife try to force the secret of goldmaking from an alchemist in this German woodcut. Torture was a perennial hazard for adepts unwilling or unable to reveal their art.

alchemist and all, into ashes.

Such stories understandably earned the puffer widespread notoriety. Indeed, so familiar a figure was the puffer in medieval life that Geoffrey Chaucer included one among the travelers whose stories are related in *The Canterbury Tales.* He did so with such realism that he aroused suspicions that he himself had been initiated into the craft. Even Elias Ashmole, the seventeenth-century scholar who included "The Canon's Yeoman's Tale" in his compendium of alchemical literature, the *Theatrum Chemicum Britannicum,* saw fit to rank Chaucer "amongst the Hermetick Philosophers . . . and one that fully knew the Mistery."

Beyond the inept or well-intentioned puffers were the clever and unscrupulous ones who were quick to accommodate any greedy citizens with get-rich-quick schemes. Not the least of these investors were the crowned heads of Europe, many of whom would gladly pay a team of alchemists in the hope of filling the royal treasury or financing their frequent wars.

James IV of Scotland, whose reign straddled the end of the fifteenth century and the start of the sixteenth, had a more than mercenary interest in alchemy, for he was as eager to expand his own knowledge as he was to enrich his treasury. Fascinated by the alchemical arts, James spared no expense in his quest for the stone (known in his court as the "quintiscence," or *quinta essentia),* and he often worked alongside his hired puffers. The royal treasurer's accounts show a profusion of disbursements, not only for the wages of his various alchemists but for all kinds of apparatus and huge quantities of fuel and raw materials. Such munificence did not go unnoticed by the puffers of the realm, who beat a path to the castle door.

The name that appears more often than any other in the accounts is that of John Damian, a personable French surgeon—or, in the parlance of the period, a leech, so called for the common medical practice of using leeches to suck blood from patients. Beginning in 1501, Damian shows up in the royal books as Maister John the French Leich. Those same accounts reveal that in addition to tapping the royal till as the king's alchemist in chief, the resourceful leech also bled the treasury in the role of His Majesty's card and gaming partner.

Under Damian's supervision, the furnaces at Stirling Castle burned day and night; yet for all the puffing, they apparently did not produce a single ounce of gold. Nonetheless, James never wavered in his loyalty to Damian. In fact, he provided the royal puffer with all the comforts of his regal home, right down to lambskin-lined gowns, linen sheets, and a tapestried bed. Damian clearly was a likable scoundrel, and a man of adventurous spirit, too, which may help explain James's forbearance. In 1509, for instance, Damian decided he could win an impromptu race from Scotland to France against a group of diplomats by flying there. Equipping himself with a pair of homemade feathered

A startled alchemist recoils from a sudden burst of smoke in this seventeenth-century Dutch painting. Fire and explosion were ever-present perils of the laboratory because alchemists frequently dealt with chemicals whose properties were not yet fully understood.

Author of forty-nine scientific books, Elizabethan alchemist John Dee resented his reputation as "a companion of the hellhounds, a caller and a conjuror of wicked and damned spirits." In his later years, Dee's image was further sullied by his alliance with Edward Kelley (opposite).

wings, Damian climbed onto the ramparts of Stirling Castle and pushed himself off into the wind. The flight was brief, for, as a later historian observed, "shortlie he fell to the ground and brak his thee bane." Undaunted, and with only the broken thigh bone as a price for his folly, Damian blamed the swift downfall on his use of hen feathers. Had he used eagle feathers, he explained, the bird's natural tendency to soar would surely have carried him safely to his destination. Damian stayed on the royal payroll until the death of his benefactor in 1512.

On the other hand, royal patronage often turned out to be a mixed blessing, both for the patron and for the patronized. Many patrons were bankrupted by unscrupulous alchemists' seemingly insatiable need for equipment and raw materials. The stakes were higher yet for the alchemists, however, since even some very patient patrons would sooner or later demand tangible results to justify all the expenses. When those results were not forthcoming, the luckier alchemists could expect imprisonment. Less fortunate puffers, such as those foolish enough to fleece Frederick, the seventeenth-century duke of Württemberg, were tortured and sometimes executed. On at least one occasion, in fact, the vengeful Frederick gathered members of his court to watch from his gold-covered grandstand as a miserable puffer was horribly tortured and then hanged on a gallows fashioned from the iron he had been unable to transmute into gold.

Queen Elizabeth I of England also had dealings with alchemists, mainly in the person of John Dee, a celebrated sixteenth-century philosopher and scientist. Described by a biographer as "one of the ornaments of his Age," Dee became an original fellow of Trinity College, Cambridge, in 1546, and later served as astrologer to Elizabeth's predecessor, Mary Tudor. He amassed one of England's finest private libraries, advised navigators, including Sir Walter Raleigh, on the geography of the New World, and was influential in fostering the rise of mathematics as a science in England. In 1558, in his capacity as royal astrologer, Dee was asked to choose the most propitious date for the coronation of Elizabeth, and he subsequently tutored the new queen in the understanding of his own mystical writings.

Nevertheless, Dee's brilliant career would take a steep downward turn. The agent responsible for his dramatic decline was one of the most incorrigible alchemical frauds of his time, Edward Kelley.

Their bizarre story begins in the 1570s, when Kelley, a lawyer who had previously been convicted for forging land deals, acquired an old parchment dealing with the transmutation of metals. He bought the document, along with two vials of powder, from a lowlife innkeeper who said they had come from the grave of a rich bishop.

Although Kelley was educated enough to read the parchment's Old Gaelic text, he lacked the knowledge of alchemy that would allow him to make use of it. In a burst of bravura, Kelley decided that the eminent John Dee, known to have an interest in the occult, would be just the man to help him with the alchemy and also to lend credibility to his schemes. A rogue of persuasive charm, Kelley got

Dee interested in his manuscript and coaxed him into the laboratory to attempt a transmutation. To Dee's intense surprise and delight, so the story goes, the experiment worked. In December 1579, they reportedly turned a pound of lead into a pound of gold.

This well-publicized success with furnace and crucible brought the pair to the attention of a certain Prince Albertus Alasco, a Polish nobleman who was a guest at Elizabeth's court. By then, the unscrupulous Kelley had tricked the honest philosopher into an iniquitous collaboration. Before ever meeting Kelley, Dee had experienced what he believed to be an encounter with the angel Uriel, during which the angel gave him the power to communicate with beings on other astral planes. When Kelley claimed that angels were speaking to him, Dee apparently did not doubt him. The two presented a séance for the benefit of Alasco and convinced him that angels said the prince was destined to become the king of Poland. With telepathic exuberance, they further informed Alasco that he would live forever.

Pleased with what he had been told, and hoping to profit from the pair's alchemical pursuits, the grateful prince invited the conspirators to his native Poland. In 1583, the unlikely pair accepted Alasco's offer and with their families set up housekeeping in the prince's castle in Cracow. There, financed by the gullible Alasco, the alchemical duo experimented without regard for cost, producing plenty of smoke but offering Alasco no gold in return. Not until he had paid over a goodly share of his fortune did the prince realize he was being swindled. Then, in 1585, he packed the unwanted houseguests out of his life.

Kelley and Dee and their families made their way to Prague, at that time one of two capitals of the Holy Roman Empire. The mystically inclined emperor Rudolf II was widely known to give a generous welcome to alchemists, but soon after the Englishmen arrived, they were alarmed to hear gossip alleging that they were involved in fraud and necromancy. They prudently left town in May 1586 and three weeks later learned that the papal nuncio had ordered Rudolf to deport them. They took refuge with a powerful nobleman, Count Rosenberg of Bohemia, who obtained official permission for them to take up residence in his castle for as long as they liked.

Despite their difficulties, Dee seems to have remained enthralled by Kelley—but not without exception. In 1587, Kelley claimed that the angel Uriel told him that henceforth he and Dee were to share "their two wives in common." Dee, whose wife was prettier and younger than Kelley's, is said to have drawn the line at this proposal. These differences precipitated a temporary disruption of his relationship with Kelley.

By 1589, a dispirited and discredited Dee returned to England, where he was promptly visited by Elizabeth I and awarded a license to practice alchemy. But there was to be no end to his misfortune. Some years later, his superb library and cherished laboratory were destroyed by a mob that had become convinced he was in league with the devil. He died in poverty at the age of eighty-one.

Kelley's fate is not so certain. One story says he was imprisoned somewhere on the Continent and fell to his death in 1597,

Alchemist, counterfeiter, medium, and sometime fraud, John Dee's partner Edward Kelley (left) also dabbled in necromancy. One account records that Kelley made a prediction by exhuming a recently buried corpse and claiming to draw prophetic utterances from its lips.

while trying to escape from a window on a rope twisted from bed linen.

It is unfortunate for Kelley and Dee that they did not gain the confidence of Rudolf II. During his reign, Prague was recognized as "the metropolis of alchemy." Here, at any time, more than 200 alchemists might be hard at work, many of them within a stone's throw of the palace on a street so crammed with laboratories that it was known as Golden Lane. Sooner or later, in fact, any puffer who was worth his mettle would find his way to Prague or would be summoned there by royal edict. Included in the latter group was an unassuming goldsmith, known only as Gustenhover, who hailed from Strasbourg and who received one of Rudolf's heavy-handed invitations after the emperor got word that the smith not only was working gold but was making it as well.

Holy Roman Emperor Rudolf II and his court visit the laboratory of an aged alchemist in this eighteenth-century Czech painting. A notable patron of alchemy and other occult arts, Rudolf collected such mystical objects as the table bell below, which is said to include all seven of the Hermetic metals.

Gustenhover was arrested and taken to Rudolf, who ordered his subject to reveal his formula for the stone. The goldsmith pleaded ignorance and explained that the powder he had used to make gold had been a thank-you gift from a mysterious stranger named Hirschborgen, who had supposedly taken shelter in Gustenhover's house during a time of personal crisis.

Rudolf, by now used to hearing such lame excuses from tight-lipped alchemists, was unconvinced and insisted that Gustenhover set to work transmuting base metals into gold. The goldsmith protested that he had only a limited supply of the philosophers' stone and no idea how to make more once it was exhausted. Then, seeing that Rudolf was determined to get his way, Gustenhover attempted to flee, but he was caught and imprisoned for life in Prague's infamous White Tower.

Even as Gustenhover and all the other puffers of Prague were laboring to find gold in their crucibles and curry favor with Rudolf II, the course of alchemy was beginning to change. The shift was subtle, and it would take more than a century to develop into the clear-cut precursor of medical science that it became. But its beginning is indelibly associated with the career of the sixteenth-century Swiss-German physician and alchemist who called himself Paracelsus.

In many ways, he seems an unlikely candidate for the heavy laurels he carries as one of the foremost alchemists of his age. A slightly built and nervous man, Paracelsus was nearly bald and in general presented so feminine an appearance that his detractors claimed, though without proof, that he had been emasculated as an infant. He had a sharp tongue and caused such controversy wherever he went that he seldom was able to hold down a position for more than a year. Although his writings were revered by succeeding generations of alchemists, he was more physician than adept, and he seems to have

Little changed in appearance from its sixteenth-century heyday, Golden Lane in Prague once housed scores of alchemists, occultists, and quacks who were attracted by the open purse of Emperor Rudolf II. Goldsmiths and jewelers supported by Rudolf could also be found in the cramped quarters that fronted the cobbled lane.

spent comparatively little time in the laboratory. Apparently he published few books during his forty-eight years, and many of the volumes that had been attributed to him after his death, particularly the alchemical tracts, were later proved to be forgeries.

Yet such was his stature even in his own lifetime that Paracelsus was called *Lutherus medicorum,* "the Luther of physicians." Historically, what he did was make alchemy, as he described it, not just "the foundation and pillar of medicine" but "that without which no physician can be a physician." Paracelsus is credited with starting to build the science of chemistry on the footings of alchemy, and through his development and use of chemically prepared medicines, he established a basis for the study of pharmacy. One present-day scholar has cited him "as the first modern medical scientist, as the precursor of microchemistry, antisepsis, modern wound surgery, homeopathy and a number of other ultra-modern achievements."

This paragon was born in the tiny Swiss village of Einsiedeln in 1493, and was given the ponderous name of Philippus Aureolus Theophrastus Bombast von Hohenheim. His father was a country doctor, and when his mother died while Theophrastus was still a boy, father and son moved in 1502 to Villach, a small river town in southern Austria where mining was a major industry. The boy was studious, and he attended a school for mining overseers and analysts that gave him firsthand experience in the metallurgical processes of the time, as well as insights into the diseases endemic to miners.

In 1507, when he was just fourteen, the young man left home and as one of a legion of wandering scholars made stops at a number of universities. None seems to have impressed the youth favorably, and with his usual sarcasm he was later to marvel at how "the high colleges managed to produce so many high asses."

Nevertheless, the scholar continued his own studies at other "high colleges" and was said to have obtained his degree as a medical doctor from the University of Ferrara in 1516, although evidence that he ever did in fact obtain this degree is not solid. It was apparently during this time, too, that the newly fledged physician shed his long list of names and rechristened himself Paracelsus, taking the name from "para-Celsus," meaning "beyond Celsus," a reference to the celebrated first-century Roman physician and a reflection of the young doctor's high opinion of himself. His low opinion of the higher education system had not changed, however. "The universities do not teach all things," he is said to have grumbled, "so a doctor must seek out old wives, gypsies, sorcerers, wandering tribes, old robbers, and such outlaws and take lessons from them. A doctor must be a traveler."

Taking his own advice, Paracelsus soon put his back to Ferrara and resumed his travels. During the next five years he claimed to have visited virtually every country in Europe, deepening his knowledge of medicine and expanding his understanding of alchemy at every stop. Later, he apparently served as an army surgeon in the Netherlands, Denmark, and Italy and eventually roamed through the Middle East before returning to Europe. In 1526, after again hopscotching across Europe, he settled briefly in Strasbourg, on the threshold of fame.

Not long afterward, he was called to Basel to treat a renowned scholar and printer named Johann Froben, whose right leg had become grossly infected. Other doctors had failed to cure the infection and were threatening amputation. Paracelsus managed to save the limb, however, and news of his success swept through the city. He made friends with important citizens, including the Dutch humanist Erasmus, who assisted in getting Paracelsus appointed as Basel's official physician, a post that also included a position as lecturer at the local university. He was just thirty-three years old and was beginning to earn his reputation as the "Luther of physicians."

Just as, ten years earlier, Martin Luther had nailed to the Wittenberg church door the theses that would be the foundation of Protestantism, Paracelsus now pinned his lecture program to the university's notice board and began to

Uncapping a flask of unknown contents, sixteenth-century alchemist Paracelsus leans on a representation of the Jewish Cabala in a frontispiece to a German treatise (right). The numbered squares beside him are also drawn from cabalistic lore, which was one of many mystical influences on Paracelsian doctrines.

attract to Basel students from all over Europe. He also touched off a storm of controversy. It started when he made the bold announcement that his lectures would be based on his own experiences as a physician and on his own methods, rather than on the timeworn teachings of such accepted authorities as Hippocrates and the second-century Greek physician Galen.

In an effort to underscore his disdain for those authorities, Paracelsus took advantage of the traditional bonfire held on Saint John's Day to burn the works of Galen and of another revered "Prince of Physicians"—the eleventh-century Islamic sage Avicenna. Paracelsus made his daring gesture so that, as he put it, "all this misery may go in the air with the smoke." In doing so, he again invited comparison to Martin Luther, who some six years earlier had brazenly torched the papal bull that threatened him with excommunication.

Paracelsus made things worse by choosing to lecture in his native German rather than the customary Latin. But perhaps most offensive to his enemies among conservative professors and physicians of Basel was his heretical message. For example, Paracelsus preached that illnesses were not the result of an imbalance of the four humors, as the ancients had theorized, but were caused by "seeds" of disease that attacked particular organs of the body. Moreover, Paracelsus declared, those illnesses could be cured through the use of chemically prepared medicines; however, this would work only if the physician first understood the relationship between the patient, the cosmos, and God. An essential key to that understanding lay in the study of alchemy, without which, as he later wrote, a doctor is nothing more than "a mixer of pig-wash trying to be a chef . . . a mere boiler of stew."

At the heart of Paracelsus's beliefs lay his view that each human being, representing the microcosm, was ineluctably linked to the cosmos, or macrocosm, and that whatever had an effect upon the one would have a similar effect upon the other. Health emanated from God, the "Great Physician," and sickness, as Paracelsus saw it, was merely a breakdown in the celestial harmony that normally exists between nature and humankind, or macrocosm and microcosm. To restore health, the physician had to restore the balance through the use of chemical remedies, which he called arcana. In these works the physician-alchemist also was compelled to rely on mediation of such influences as the rays of stars and what Paracelsus called vaguely "the breath of the Lord."

Paracelsus acknowledged his belief in the Greek concept of the four elements, but he also averred that on another level the cosmos was fashioned from three spiritual substances—the so-called trinity of mercury, sulfur, and salt—which he named the three principles, or *tria prima.*

These three substances, according to Paracelsus, gave every object its inner essence and outward form. Highly flammable sulfur lent matter a fiery, active presence while salt was responsible for solidity and color, and mercury accounted for an object's vaporous quality. This alchemical trinity defined the human identity as well. Sulfur embodied the soul, which was seen to be the emotions and desires; salt represented the body; mercury epitomized the spirit, comprising imagination, moral judgment, and the higher mental faculties.

For Paracelsus, the connection between these attributes and alchemy was obvious. Only by understanding the chemical nature of the tria prima could a physician discover the precise arcana needed to cure a specific disease. Thus the true mission of alchemy was not to pursue gold and silver but to be the handmaiden to medicine. And although, like most adepts, Paracelsus believed alchemy was "truly a gift from God" and a mystical as well as a chemical process, it was in the practical application of alchemy's store of technical data that he made his most important contributions.

He was one of the first to catch a glimmer of the true nature of the circulation of blood, which he called the sap of life. More than a century later, William Harvey, the scientist credited with the discovery of blood circulation, would use a similar analogy. Paracelsus was also among the first phy-

sicians to treat epilepsy as a disease and not as a symptom of demonic possession or as proof of lunacy. Moreover, he made the connection between the so-called miner's disease, today known as silicosis, and the inhalation of metal vapors. Until then, its victims had been informed that their suffering had been meted out by mountain spirits as a punishment for sin.

Paracelsus left an even more important legacy by adding compounds containing sulfur, mercury, and iron to the physician's medicine chest. It was Paracelsus, for example, who not only described the causes, symptoms, and diagnosis of syphilis but also specified the first treatment that relied on precisely measured doses of mercury compounds taken orally by the patient. Almost 400 years later, at the dawn of the twentieth century, a similar treatment was still being prescribed for syphilis.

Paracelsus's alchemical research in pursuit of the elixir of life also led him to extract the quinta essentia of the poppy. The result was the discovery of laudanum, an opium derivative that Paracelsus prescribed as a painkiller in the form of "three black pills." And by combining alcohol and sulfuric acid, he prepared etherlike drugs that could be used to induce sleep.

These teachings attracted an avid following of students to Paracelsus's lectures in Basel, but they also earned him the violent antipathy of other students, of the faculty, and of most of the city's good burghers. He did not help his cause by sneering at his fellow physicians. "Let me tell you this," he apostrophized in one oft-quoted address, "every little hair on my neck knows more than you and all your scribes, and my shoebuckles are more learned than your Galen and Avicenna, and my beard has more experience than all your high colleges."

This bravado was more than Basel could bear. And when he became embroiled in a lawsuit with a patient who refused to pay his bill, Paracelsus knew it was time to leave town. Once again, the physician who liked to think of himself as a simple "wayfarer" was adrift. Ahead lay a journey

In this woodcut from a treatise attributed to Paracelsus, a Renaissance infirmary run according to Paracelsian principles provides its patients with rest, a healthful diet, and loving care.

Paving the Way to Modern Medicine

Mystical in temperament and relying more on intuition than on the results of clinical studies, the Swiss-German alchemist Paracelsus was by no means a physician in the modern sense. Yet his approach to healing, which emphasized careful diagnosis, humane care of the patient, and the idea that the cause of disease could originate outside the body, marked the beginning of a revolution in Western medicine.

Rejecting the stale medieval dogma that all disease was caused by internal imbalances of blood, phlegm, and two varieties of bile, Paracelsus contended that illnesses could come from external "seeds"—not far removed from the modern concept of germs. After his death, alchemists such as Robert Fludd continued to propagate similar ideas in treatises and in engravings like the one at far right.

To determine which seeds had attacked which parts of the body, Paracelsus stressed the importance of examining the patient—considered unnecessary by most physicians of the time. In addition, he encouraged the use of laboratory tests, including the chemical analysis of urine through distillation *(right).* Although patients were then treated according to their diagnosis, they were also subject to a regimen of rest, good food, and gentle care *(above)*—measures still emphasized in medical and nursing schools today.

Before Paracelsus, urinalysis was based solely on color, conveniently tabulated in circular charts like the one above. Whitish urine, for example, was thought to indicate malaria, vertigo, or alcoholism.

One of Paracelsus's urinalysis procedures involved distilling urine in an anatomical furnace of his own design (below). This procedure, he believed, would show what part of the body was most afflicted and even identify the disease itself.

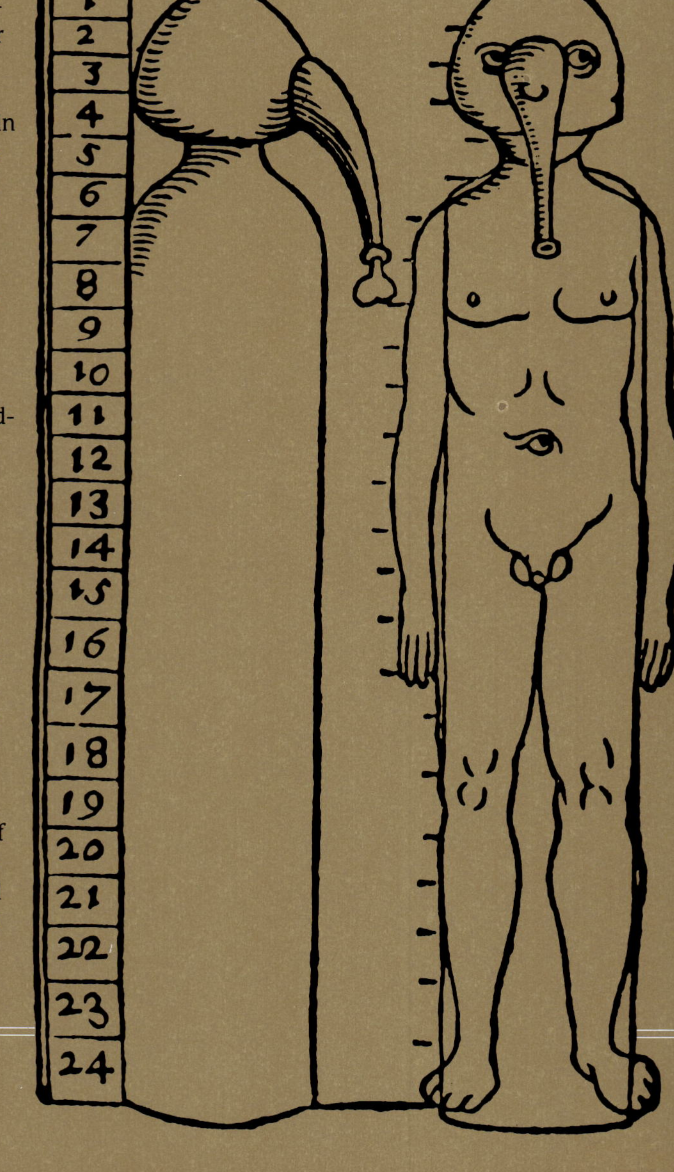

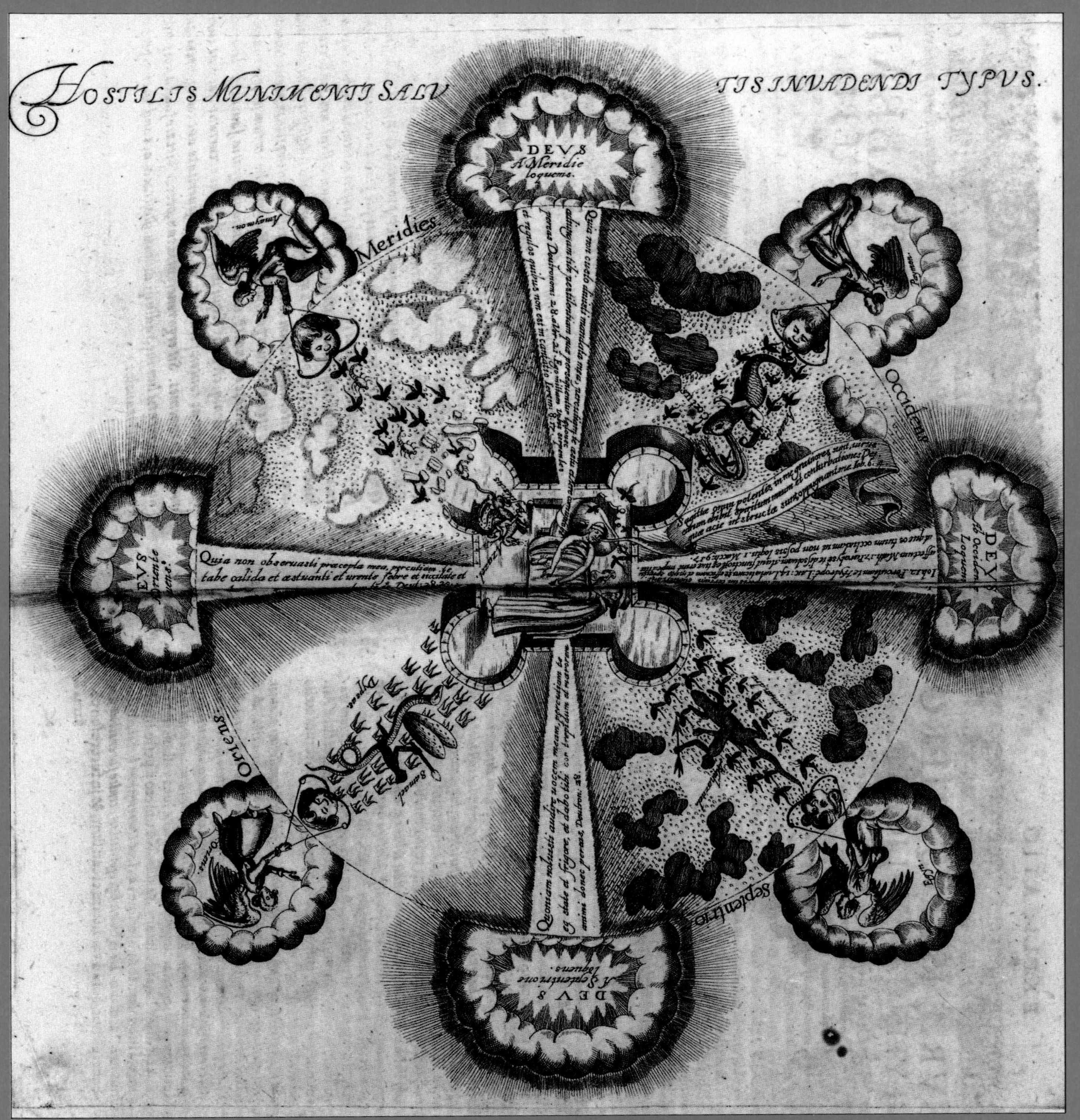

In a Robert Fludd engraving, four winds blow against a patient's "fortress of health," already invaded by pestilence in the broken turret at upper left. Alchemy was among the first healing systems to emphasize that agents from outside the body could cause disease.

In an engraving inspired by Johann Goethe's nineteenth-century drama Faust, the spectacled title character creates a living homunculus, or little man, in a vessel heated at his own hearth. For centuries, the alchemical creation of such artificial human beings captured the imagination of artists and authors alike.

An alchemical couple react in astonishment upon seeing a flask containing a newly formed homunculus in this Dutch painting from the seventeenth century. To their evident shock, arcane procedures that have been taken from the texts strewn across their table have granted the dimly seen creature the spark of life.

that took him from country to country; over the next thirteen years he would reside in no fewer than sixty-two different places.

During these years of wandering, he produced a volume called *Greater Surgery;* it appeared in 1536. The book helped restore his reputation and make him a hero to a whole new generation of physicians.

Combining modern technology with alchemical tradition, seventeenth-century experimenter Niklaas Hartsoeker engraved this image of a homunculus incubating in a human sperm. Sperm was a key ingredient in the Paracelsian recipe for the homunculus, which supposedly required no ovum to come to fruition.

But he would be taken to task by future critics for his espousal of a belief that enjoyed wide currency in his time—the idea that an artificial human called a homunculus could be created through an alchemical process. Paracelsus's own recipe entailed putting human semen into an airtight jar, burying the container in horse manure for forty days, and then magnetizing it. By then the homunculus was supposed to be alive and moving, though invisible. The alchemist would keep it at the temperature of a mare's womb for forty weeks while feeding it human blood. At the end of that time it would resemble a perfect but tiny human child. "It may be raised and educated like any other child," said Paracelsus, "until it grows older and is able to look after itself." Needless to say, there is no evidence to indicate that Paracelsus ever succeeded in creating a homunculus.

His wanderings ultimately took him to Salzburg in Austria, where he died in 1541. Even his death was a source of controversy. While some said the doctor expired quietly after a brief illness, detractors claimed that he had gotten drunk and fallen down a flight of stairs. Others countered that Paracelsus had been assassinated, and, predictably, a few suggested that the alchemist had not died at all but had found the elixir of life and given himself a dose of immortality.

He was interred among the poor at a local cemetery. On top of his grave lay a stone bearing an inscription that expressed both his contempt for this life and his hope for a better one in a hereafter. "Vitam cum morte mutavit," it read. "He exchanged death for life."

Ambulating slowly with a walker, a forlorn homunculus appears at the edge of a triptych by sixteenth-century Dutch painter Hieronymus Bosch. Mature homunculi like this one were thought to need little supervision.

Paracelsus had prophesied a kind of immortality for himself. "When I am dead," he predicted, "my teachings will live." And so they did, inspiring generations of alchemists and doctors to change the way medicine worked. Yet no man can be given the whole credit for the shape of such a major intellectual movement, and many commentators have noted that the parts of Paracelsus's alchemical achievements seem to be less than the sum of his overall influence. It may be that in the end the most important boon the controversial Paracelsus made to science was that he himself served as a kind of human philosophers' stone, a radical catalyst for change at a time when revolution was in the air. Such a judgment would befit a man whose personal motto was "Let no one who can be his own belong to another."

Alchemical Wisdom from a Wordless Book

For practitioners of a secret art, alchemists have always been surprisingly eager to commit their methods to paper. But their treatises, while numerous, are in no way easily comprehensible. Alchemist-authors have traditionally veiled their writings under layers of metaphor, symbol, and allusion intended to conceal hard-won knowledge from all but the most persistent readers.

This deliberate obscurity reached a climax in the *Mutus Liber* (Wordless Book), a recipe for the philosophers' stone in which enigmatic pictures almost entirely replaced conventional text. First printed in France in 1677, this anonymous guide to the so-called great work was reissued in 1702 in the fifteen-plate edition shown at right and on the pages that follow.

THE SLEEPER AWAKENS

In a vision reminiscent of Jacob's dream of a ladder extending to heaven, angels summon the sleeping alchemist to begin creating the philosophers' stone. The Mutus Liber derives its name from the Latin inscription on this plate. It begins: "The wordless book, in which nevertheless the whole of Hermetic Philosophy is set forth." Directly below are three biblical citations, written backward in a flourish of alchemical cryptography. The first—21. 11. 82. Neg:—corresponds to Genesis 28:11-12, the story of Jacob's ladder. The other two passages concern the divine origins of dew—the prima materia, or initial ingredient, of the alchemical process. A border of thorny rose branches suggests that the work ahead will be beautiful but considerably difficult.

Three centuries of scholars have puzzled over the *Mutus Liber* without producing a definitive interpretation. Many of the book's images can be plausibly explained in several ways, and some picture sequences simply outline general processes, leaving the exact details to the intuition of the would-be adept. The most frustrating riddle may be the yet-to-be-interpreted fourteenth plate *(page 77),* which addresses the crucial final steps in forming the philosophers' stone but provides only the sketchiest of directions.

The partial interpretation of the *Mutus Liber* provided here follows the work of Adam McLean, a modern English Hermeticist. In true alchemist's fashion, McLean has stated frankly that he would not provide a fuller explanation even if he could, because he believes that the mystery of such venerable texts is the source of their continuing power. Instead, students of the *Mutus Liber* must supply the missing details for themselves, relying on a combination of spiritual insight and diligent study.

A LOOK AHEAD

In the first of three similar plates interspersed throughout the book, an allegorical scene of deities and angels provides a broad hint as to the nature of the work to come. In this instance, the sea god Neptune, contained in a sealed flask, shelters childlike spirits representative of the sun and moon. This grouping suggests that the alchemist must produce a watery fluid—signified by Neptune—to be combined with solar and lunar essences. In the laboratory scene at the bottom of the plate, male and female alchemists—sometimes interpreted as the two opposing aspects of a single alchemist's character—gaze prayerfully at their furnace. The two curtains hanging behind them suggest mysteries that have yet to be revealed.

THE ALCHEMIST'S COSMOS

Before examining the physical process of making the philosophers' stone, the Mutus Liber provides one final preparatory diagram, which places the work in its larger spiritual context. In this macrocosmic view, the benevolent Zeus is astride an eagle as he watches over nested circles representing the heavens, the earth, and the oceans. The alchemical couple appears twice: once fishing from a rowboat; and again below in the earthly sphere, where the man fishes for a mermaid and his partner holds a birdcage. According to Adam McLean, this scene implies that the alchemist must come to terms with spiritual forces from the waters of the earth and with those from the heavens.

COMMENCING THE GREAT WORK

As their labors begin, the two alchemists wring dew from cloths they have stretched across posts in a meadow. The most propitious timing for this process is indicated by the presence of the ram and bull in the middle distance. The animals probably represent the zodiacal periods of Aries and Taurus—late March to late May. A cascade of celestial rays suggests the etheric forces some alchemists believe are incorporated in dew, which they view as an elemental liquid, formed from air and found on solid earth.

DISTILLING THE DEW

Back in the laboratory, the alchemists boil the dew in their furnace, then capture the resulting vapors as they condense. In the center panel, the female alchemist scrapes up the solid residues and hands them to the god Saturn, shown carrying one of his children. In many alchemical texts, Saturn represents lead. In this case, however, the lunar crescent on the god's chest probably indicates that the residues are supposedly a mixture of lead and lunar essence. In the bottom panel, the alchemists pour the liquid distillate into four containers to be repeatedly evaporated and condensed—a process known as circulation. The number 40, faintly

EXTRACTING SOLAR ESSENCE

Having circulated the dew distillate for the prescribed length of time, the alchemists empty it into a jar, which is then heated in a water bath. In the center panel, the male alchemist draws off a second distillate and his partner once again retrieves the residue—this time symbolized by a flower that strangely resembles some modern diagrams of molecular structure. Below, the residue is passed to the sun god Apollo and thus is symbolically identified as solar essence. The couple then resume work on the lunar-lead residue left from the first distillation, heating it in a crucible to dry it out.

EXTRACTING LUNAR ESSENCE

The second liquid distillate is now combined with the dried lunar-lead residue, which the female alchemist stirs and crushes with a pestle. After storing this mixture for an indefinite period, the alchemists heat it in a shallow pan (center panel), and the woman spoons off the residues, which are now designated as lunar essence by the little stars on their container. In the bottom panel, the Mutus Liber artist reviews the process with an allegorical reenactment. First, Saturn, who has come to represent the lunar-lead residue, is heated on a fire—just as the residue itself was heated. Then, the male alchemist pours distillate over the god, washing him free of the lunar essence; this parallels the steps shown at the top of the plate. Finally, Saturn presents the newly created lunar essence to Luna, goddess of the moon.

PLANNING THE NEXT PHASE

A second allegorical plate presents the next stage of the alchemists' work. At the top, Mercury has replaced Neptune in the flask held aloft by the angels. This suggests that the alchemists will now be working with rain, or "mercurial water," rather than with dew. Below the flask, two flocks of birds bear the symbols of the solar and lunar essences already derived. By showing these symbols in conjunction with Mercury, the Mutus Liber artist has anticipated a process in which the essences will be brought back together in the medium of mercurial water. Meanwhile, in the laboratory below, the curtains have been drawn to the sides, exposing a pair of windows; these symbolize the spiritual and practical insights gained by the adepts thus far. Some of the wall is still concealed, though, suggesting the alchemists have far to go before all is revealed.

GATHERING RAINWATER

Going out to the meadows as they did when gathering the dew, the alchemical couple now collect rainwater, captured in shallow pans. The ram and bull again dominate the pastures, suggesting that the second phase of the work also must await the advantageous zodiacal alignments of springtime. At bottom, the alchemists consolidate the water they have harvested, and the woman offers it to Mercury.

SUN AND MOON REUNITED

In the images at the top of this plate, the alchemical couple recombine the lunar and solar essences—designated by the star and the flower—measuring out equal parts of each before diluting them with rainwater. At center, the male alchemist seals the solution in a glass flask, then places it in the furnace. Below, an allegorical recapitulation of the process shows Luna and Apollo—representing the lunar and solar essences—hand in hand beside the furnace. The number 10 at the feet of both deities suggests that the heating must be carried on for ten days. An egg depicted in cross section at the far left of the panel is a traditional symbol of the philosophers' stone, which is the ultimate target, or objective, of the alchemists.

BEGINNING THE FINAL STAGE

A third allegorical plate introduces the final stage of the alchemical process. As in the similar composition three plates earlier, the bird to the right of the flask carries a symbol of lunar essence. Its counterpart on the left, however, now holds a symbol capped with a bar, a sign that the solar essence has been modified, or combined with other substances. In the panel below, the laboratory curtains have now disappeared entirely, revealing four windows through which the alchemists can survey and comprehend the world. But for the moment, they are still intent on the work before them.

BACK TO THE MEADOW

For a final time, the alchemists obtain their raw materials from nature, once again collecting rainwater. Little has changed from the previous meadow scene: The ram and the bull remain at loggerheads, and the collected fluid is again delivered to Mercury. Adam McLean suggests such repetition is in itself significant, since alchemical texts rarely repeat ideas. For him, the similarity between this plate and its earlier analogue implies that the work to come will continue to involve a repetitive process.

A LIQUID MULTIPLICATION

As they did after their previous trip to the meadow, the alchemists combine equal portions of two substances with rainwater, seal the mixture in a flask, and heat it in the furnace. This time, however, the two primary ingredients are lunar essence and the material produced in the previous phase of the work—the latter denoted by the symbol of a sun with a tiny human face. The scene at the bottom includes a series of increasingly large numbers, leading to infinity. This may mean that the dilution process is to be repeated until all of the supplies—including the rainwater—have been depleted.

THE PHILOSOPHERS' STONE

The Mutus Liber's pictorial explanation of the great work culminates in this cryptic series of images. The three furnaces in the top panel, along with the three human figures in the panel below, can be taken as another recapitulation of the entire alchemical process. In the second panel, the male and female adepts are joined by a child, who may be executing the final steps of forming the philosophers' stone. The third panel probably hints obliquely at details of the child's actions, but its exact meaning is elusive. In the bottom panel, a flask containing the philosophers' stone is flanked by the successful

THE SPIRIT TRANSFORMED

In a spiritual triumph that parallels their material success in creating the philosophers' stone, the alchemists ascend directly to the celestial realm, exclaiming, "Provided with eyes, thou departest." Below them lies a dying Hercules, a mythological figure who—like the alchemists—was drawn bodily into heaven. Jacob's ladder, no longer needed, lies abandoned in the background. And in place of the thorny rose branches that decorated the book's title page, now there are boughs from a fruit tree, the reward for persistence and dedication.

CHAPTER 3

Into the Scientific Era

sensational story began circulating in the spring of 1782 among the learned members of the Royal Society of London for Improving Natural Knowledge. One of their own, a thirty-year-old fellow of the society and chemist named James Price, was claiming to have solidified mercury and then to have turned it into pure gold.

According to contemporary accounts, Price performed similar feats on two separate occasions during the next few weeks, both times making believers of skeptical witnesses. In the first instance, he was said to use a grain of white powder to transform two ounces of mercury into twenty-nine grains of pure silver. The second demonstration was by all reports even more remarkable. Before a distinguished audience that included three members of the House of Lords, four senior Church dignitaries, and two master gold refiners, Price gave all appearances of having manufactured mercury—or quicksilver, as it was commonly known—and of converting it to gold.

Throughout the demonstration, he displayed utter confidence, urging the onlookers to scrutinize his every move. Each vessel, each instrument, every bit of material that he used, he first offered for examination. He recruited Lord Palmerston of the admiralty to weigh out half an ounce of a red powder that he identified as the gold-transmuting agent. When Price had sprinkled the powder into a crucible that contained the quicksilver, he placed it in a furnace to heat for a number of hours. At last, the chemist removed the crucible, allowed it to cool, and broke it open. Inside was a shiny yellow nugget of pure gold—its composition certified in tests conducted by the master refiners.

Back in London, members of the Royal Society could wait no longer. They asked their young colleague to appear before them with samples not only of the finished gold and silver but also of the white and red transmuting powders. Price acquiesced to the extent of sending along his homemade metals but claimed that he could not show them the powders because he had exhausted his entire supply. He insisted, moreover, that he was presently too ill and too tired to pursue any further alchemical work. The society's president, Sir Joseph Banks, pressed the matter, telling Price that he must appear in the new year and bring with him the remaining evidence. Otherwise, Banks assured him, he would face expulsion from the organization and be branded a charlatan.

Reluctantly, Price agreed to come to London for a meeting the following spring. He then withdrew to his laboratory, intent apparently on producing a new batch of the magical powders. In fact, James Price was preparing another sort of finale.

On the appointed day, as skeptics and believers alike gathered at the London headquarters of the Royal Society, Price remained sequestered at his laboratory near Guildford, composing a last will and testament. Weeks earlier, he had distilled a lethal dose of the chemical compound hydrogen cyanide. Now, he drank a glass of water scented with laurel and took a single swig of the poison. Within minutes he had collapsed to the floor and his housekeeper was rushing off in search of a doctor. But as the young chemist no doubt had expected, he was dead before help could arrive.

In a sense, James Price's desperate end can be read as a triumph of modern science over the ancient art of alchemy. In earlier times, Price might have bluffed his way through a cross-examination by his peers—and they, in any case, would probably have been more interested in the gold than in the facts. By the end of the eighteenth century, however, the foundations of modern science were well established, and skepticism toward the alchemical arts was becoming pervasive among educated men and women. Faced with the scrutiny of the cold-eyed realists who made up the membership of the Royal Society, Price may well have chosen suicide to avoid being exposed as a fraud.

In hindsight, the mid-1600s—more than a century before Price's death—stand out as a watershed in the intellectual evolution of Western society. It was a time when the balance of mainstream intellectual values began to tip away from its enduring dependence on arcane systems such as philosophical alchemy and toward a new outlook shaped by the insights and extraordinary promise of experimental science. But alchemy's decline would be gradual, and the epitaph for this ancient tradition would never be fully written.

The resilience of the Hermetic arts in the face of new scientific knowledge is not altogether surprising. For at least a century and a half after the death in 1541 of alchemy's high priest, Paracelsus, his philosophy was one of the dominant intellectual forces in Europe. Spurred on by Nicolaus Copernicus's sixteenth-century explanation of the earth's planetary system, alchemists came to believe that they were uniquely equipped to decipher a coherent understanding of nature.

In the grand view they contrived, all of life was a harmonious system of correspondences that linked the heavens to the planets, the planets to the earth, the earth to seasonal changes, the seasons to human illness, and illness to chemical medicines. It seemed entirely likely that in the long run discoveries on earth would not only eliminate human suffering but would also make plain the underlying wisdom of God's higher laws. The Paracelsians drew a broad analogy between the creation of the cosmos by the Divine Power and the alchemist's experiments in the laboratory: In both cases, the magical agency of fire was called upon to separate the pure from the impure, good

Mysticism and Christian devotion fueled the research of German alchemist Heinrich Khunrath, who sought to discover God by learning the workings of matter. In the 1602 engraving opposite, Khunrath kneels before the altar in his "laboratorium," a name made up of the Latin words meaning "work" and "a place of prayer." The Latin inscription on the ceiling beam reads, "Without Divine inspiration nobody is great."

from evil, light from darkness, and order from chaos. Within this philosophical framework, God was considered the primordial chemist, the alchemist was his disciple, and the "great work" of the adept was imbued with sacred significance.

The challenge confronting the alchemist was to unravel the skein of correspondences that bound together everything in the cosmos. It was theoretically possible to achieve this objective by studying the universe as a whole and working downward to a more specialized understanding of humankind—by moving, in other words, from the macrocosm to the microcosm. The Paracelsians saw obvious problems with this approach, however. Put simply, God in his heaven was difficult to investigate directly. Fortunately, the opposite approach offered a more manageable alternative. Since everything in the macrocosm was also to be found in precise concordance in the microcosm, they could study humanity and its place in the material world in order to comprehend the larger realm. By applying their beliefs and practices at this level, the followers of Paracelsus hoped to begin by finding cures for all illnesses and end by bringing about a spiritual regeneration that would lead to a better world.

Perhaps inevitably, this glorious vision fell victim to the breadth of its own ambition. With alchemists seeking both mundane medical innovations and cosmic revelations, the craft began to come apart at the seams and the inheritors of Paracelsus's legacy split into several camps. One group consisted of purists who carried on a search for the spirit of life on the mystical high ground of "chemical philosophy." Others gravitated to more pragmatic goals and focused mainly on experimentation in the laboratory. And—just as in every previous era—there was the usual assortment of true believers and charlatans preoccupied strictly with physical transmutation of base metals into rare ones and lusting after nothing more than wealth and power.

Yet even while their practices came under increasing fire from more-modern thinkers, the heirs of Paracelsus made an indelible mark on history. Most of the prominent seventeenth-century men who are now regarded as founders of modern science were in fact eager practitioners of the Hermetic arts. Francis Bacon, Robert Boyle, even Sir Isaac Newton—who lived well into the eighteenth century and was one of the most influential of all contemporary scientists—were serious students of alchemy (although Bacon, for one, rejected the metaphysical beliefs embraced by many adepts). Throughout most of the 1700s, the line between mystical philosophers and practical researchers was often blurred to the point of being meaningless. The alchemists who carefully compounded medical remedies in their laboratories might well retire to their libraries to pen occult tracts that today read like utter poppycock. And even the out-and-out gold seekers would occasionally stumble upon useful chemical discoveries.

Despite the fuzziness of the distinction between the "chemists" and the "philosophers," the ideological extremes of alchemical practice were broadly defined by the teachings of two sixteenth-century physicians, Peter Severinus of Denmark and Heinrich Khunrath of Saxony. Although they were

DORMIENS VIGILA.
TATVM, SVCCEDET ALIQVANDO.
FESTIN
LENTE
Maturandum
HF Vriese
pinxit.
Henricus Khunrath Lips: Theosophiæ amator & Medicinæ utriusq Doctor, DEI gratia. inventor: Paullus vander doort Ant.werp. sculpsit.

both second-generation Paracelsians, they had markedly different approaches to the goals of alchemy.

Severinus, who lived from 1542 to 1602, was personal physician to King Frederick II of Denmark and an influential figure among the adepts of his day. In 1571 he published a work called *Idea Medicinae Philosophicae*, (For the Purposes of Philosophical Medicine), which would be the standard reference on Paracelsian medicine for nearly a hundred years. With an unadorned lyricism rare for his time, Severinus advised his fellow physicians to reject their comfortable academic beliefs and get their hands dirty discovering the world by direct observation: "Sell your lands, your houses, your garments and your jewelry; burn up your books," he wrote. "On the other hand, buy yourselves stout shoes, travel to the mountains, search the valleys, the deserts, the shores of the sea, and the deepest depressions of the earth; note with care the distinctions between animals, the differences of plants, the various kinds of minerals, the properties and mode of origin of everything that exists. Be not ashamed to study diligently the astronomy and terrestrial philosophy of the peasantry. Lastly, purchase coal, build furnaces, watch and operate with the fire without wearying. In this way and no other, you will arrive at a knowledge of things and their properties."

Severinus's admonition to keep the furnaces stoked was a crucial element of the practical alchemists' creed, because heat was key to most chemical experiments and fire was thought of as the sacred facilitator. A later alchemist echoed Severinus's counsel when he exhorted his readers to "put then on the Glouves and Cuffs, for you must go to the fire, and happily to the fiery furnace."

Heinrich Khunrath, born in 1560, preached a different sermon altogether. He studied at the University of Basel, the same school in which Paracelsus had taught some sixty years earlier, and he, too, had gone on to practice medicine. But Khunrath's alchemy was spiritual rather than practical. He specifically decried any attempt to transmute mercury, for instance, as a false quest. His chief contribution was the *Amphitheatrum Sapientiae Aeternae* (The Amphitheater of Eternal Knowledge), a mystical treatise that appeared posthumously in 1609.

In the *Amphitheatrum*, Khunrath acknowledged his belief in the physical reality of the philosophers' stone and suggested that it should be used to achieve universal knowledge through spiritual refinement. He described a seven-step process for purifying the spirit—a procedure that paralleled the stages of refining base metals. Khunrath also claimed that a requirement of the final step in the alchemical process was for the adept to gain true knowledge of God and Christ. In support of this assertion, he pointed out that the process would be meaningless otherwise, since ultimately God was the moving factor behind everything in the universe. In Khunrath's view, the philosophers' stone corresponded to the presence of Jesus Christ, whom he sometimes referred to as the "Son of Macrocosm."

Just as Christ had brought wholeness to man the microcosm, so the discovery of the philosophers' stone would reveal the true nature of the macrocosm. This theme, blended with a familiar Paracelsian emphasis on macrocosm-microcosm correspondences and the use of ancient Hermetic texts, would become central to the beliefs of many alchemists besides Heinrich Khunrath. They came to see the direct knowledge of God as the proper goal of alchemy.

For all his lofty aspirations, Khunrath was not a man of great tolerance, and he was convinced that the task of enlightening humankind was not going to be easy. Most of his writings were in Latin, but in one tract he lapsed into his native German to point out testily that "he who sets out to make wise men of fools will be kept very busy." Khunrath would not have long to carry on the struggle. His efforts to put alchemy on a purely spiritual course came to an end in 1605, when he died in obscurity and poverty.

Close on the heels of Khunrath's *Amphitheatrum* was another influential seventeenth-century work, the *Fama Fraternitatis* (Fame of the Brotherhood), which began circulating in manuscript form in Germany around 1610. The *Fama* was issued anonymously—a fairly common practice in that era—but its contents left no doubt that it was written by someone steeped in alchemical tradition.

This curious document tells the story of Christian Rosenkreutz, a learned and pious man born in 1378, who had traveled for many years in strange lands mastering the secrets of medicine and nature. Possessed of the elixir of life—or so the story goes—Rosenkreutz had lived for 106 years, during which time he gathered around him a group of seven disciples. Like many of his predecessors, who passed on their secrets to a few chosen heirs, Rosenkreutz had shared his wisdom with his followers, who came to be known as the Brotherhood of the Rosy Cross. He charged them to perpetuate his legacy by passing on their knowledge to succeeding generations for the reformation of the entire world. As revealed in the *Fama,* the brotherhood went out from time to time to find a few worthy recruits, who were then initiated into the secret philosophy handed down by Rosenkreutz.

The *Fama* entreated all lovers of wisdom to reexamine the arts and sciences, searching for evidence of both truth and self-deception. And it exhorted them to make themselves available for membership in the brotherhood, should they ever be called. Readers were advised that they need not bother trying to contact the brotherhood and that it was—in any event—impossible. Perfect anonymity, it appears, was an essential feature of the Rosy Cross community. But suitable candidates could take comfort in the certainty that they would be recognized by their works and recruited in secret when the time was right. The author of the *Fama* added enticingly that membership, if and when it came, "shall be beneficial to him in goods, body, and soul"—words that seemed to promise wealth, spiritual enlightenment, and eternal life.

The *Fama* was followed in 1615 and 1616 by two other works: *Confessio Fraternitatis R.C.* (Confession of the Brotherhood of the Rosy Cross) explained the brotherhood's thirty-seven reasons for being; the later work, *The Chemical Wedding of Christian Rosenkreutz in the Year 1459,* was an allegorical tale taken by many to be a satirical attack on the false claims of alchemical gold seekers. For such people, Rosenkreutz and his brotherhood felt only disdain.

Although the three manifestoes were published anonymously, they were clearly related. And they were packed with the lore of alchemy: There were references to the Greek and Egyptian deity of the great work, Hermes Trismegistus, and reminders of the necessity of keeping arcane knowledge safely hidden from ordinary people. In addition, there was testimony to the existence of magical elixirs that made eternal life a possibility.

In true alchemical tradition, specific meanings of passages throughout these books were vexingly ambiguous—so much so that scholars would quarrel over the intentions of the authors for many years to come. Additional heat was kindled by the strong Protestant cast of the manifestoes, which raised violent antipathy among Catholics. The anger was not misplaced: One passage of the *Confessio* suggested, for example, putting a stop to the pope's "asinine brayings" by tearing him to pieces with nails.

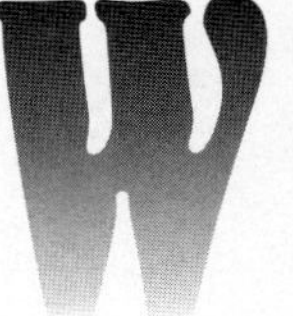

Whether the Brotherhood of the Rosy Cross ever existed is a question that has never been answered satisfactorily. Most students of the period discount as pure allegory the details of Christian Rosenkreutz's life and the foundations of the brotherhood. In a general sense, the philosophical roots of the ideas that came to be called Rosicrucianism can be found in the teachings of the great sixteenth-century alchemists Paracelsus and John Dee. But scholars have put forth theories about other sources as well. A few latter-day Hermeticists, noting similarities between the *Fama* and Francis Bacon's 1605 treatise entitled *The Advancement of Learning,* have attributed the manifestoes to him—just as some scholars have proposed that the eminent British philosopher-statesman is the true author of various Shakespearean plays.

A sober examination of Bacon's writings, however, reveals that although he read widely in alchemical literature and shared a concern over the "corruption of philosophy," he was no real believer in the metaphysical methods of the

Christian Rosenkreutz, mythical founder of the Rosicrucians and practitioner of alchemy, sits in his tomb under the philosophers' mountain in this allegorical woodcut of the late eighteenth century. The number at the bottom, 1604, is the year in which a handful of adepts supposedly discovered Rosenkreutz's perfectly preserved body in a secret tomb, 120 years after his death. An alchemist's furnace puffs smoke on one side of the mountain, opposite a tub symbolically holding the so-called essences of the sun and moon, common ingredients of alchemical recipes. The hen on its nest represents the philosopher guarding the secrets of the art.

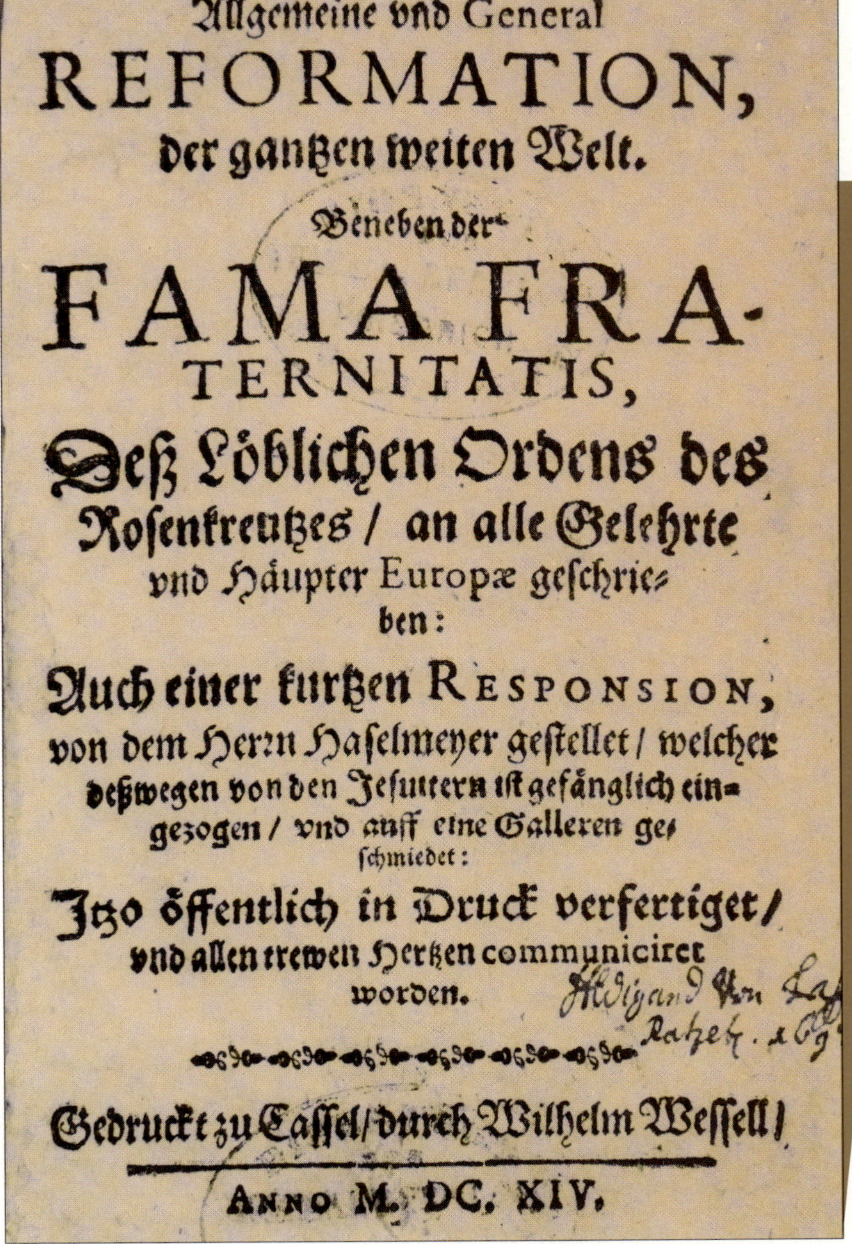
Allgemeine vnd General
REFORMATION,
der gantzen weiten Welt.
Beneben der
FAMA FRA-
TERNITATIS,
Deß Löblichen Ordens des
Rosenkreutzes / an alle Gelehrte
vnd Häupter Europæ geschrie-
ben:
Auch einer kurtzen RESPONSION,
von dem Herrn Haselmeyer gestellet / welcher
deßwegen von den Jesuitern ist gefänglich ein-
gezogen / vnd auff eine Galleren ge-
schmiedet:
Itzo öffentlich in Druck verfertiget /
vnd allen trewen Hertzen communiciret
worden.
Gedruckt zu Cassel / durch Wilhelm Wessell /
ANNO M. DC. XIV.

The title page of the Fama Fraternitatis, a 1614 book that declared the existence of the Rosicrucians, proclaims in German that the work is "Addressed to the Learned in General and the Governors of Europe" and that its goal is "Reformation of the Whole Wide World."

adepts. He accused alchemists of vanity and "extreme levity" and recommended that their efforts be suppressed because of their "unwholesome mixture of things human and divine." Sounding very much like the next generation of scientists who would be his intellectual heirs, Bacon proclaimed that the proper role of the scholar was "not to imagine or suppose, but to discover, what nature does or may be made to do." And this, he asserted, could be accomplished only by taking a hard-eyed look at reality. These were not the convictions of a follower of the Brotherhood of the Rosy Cross.

A more likely source of Rosicrucianism is to be found in a circle of learned academics who studied at the Bavarian University of Tübingen in the early 1600s. Led by a law professor named Christoph Besold, these men met with one another over a period of years and may well have launched the fantasy of a utopian brotherhood as a way of promoting their own Protestant solutions to the bitter religious and intellectual conflicts of their era. One of their number, Johann Valentin Andreae, later claimed to have had a hand in writing the *Chemical Wedding,* although he expressed some embarrassment over his role in what he described as a youthful folly. Whether or not the book was originally written as a prank, Andreae eventually came to be a strong believer in spiritual alchemy.

As for the shadowy brotherhood itself, history holds no credible proof that an actual fraternity existed at the time the Rosicrucian manifestoes were published or in the decades that followed. Many intellectuals, especially alchemists, attempted to contact the Rosy Cross brothers, but there is no record of anyone who succeeded. This cannot, of course, be taken as proof of their nonexistence, since total secrecy was part of the supposed Rosicrucian creed. The French scientist and philosopher René Descartes was one of the many who tried vainly to woo the attention of the brotherhood. When he failed, he concluded that the fraternity did not exist.

Wherever the Rosy Cross manifestoes came from, there is no doubt whatever that Rosicrucianism took wings across northern Europe. In the decade after the *Fama* first appeared, it was answered by scores of books and pamphlets debating the merits of Rosicrucian doctrine and the validity of spiritual alchemy. And even if there was no earthly brotherhood, there was certainly no shortage of vol-

unteers who were willing to answer the call. One of the first to offer his services was Michael Maier, the personal physician to Emperor Rudolf II of Hungary. Maier had longstanding interest in alchemy and was well known for the receptiveness he displayed toward just about anyone claiming to have insight into the secrets of the great work. His open-mindedness was shared by his employer the emperor, who was said to have spent the lion's share of his wealth subsidizing self-proclaimed adepts. Upon reading the *Fama,* Maier was so taken with the promises of the Rosicrucians that he set out to meet a genuine Rosy Cross brother. He traveled from city to city, generating interest in the secret fraternity wherever he went. When he failed to establish contact, he apparently decided to form a satellite organization in which he would be the first initiate. His enthusiasm seems to have been contagious, for many other would-be Rosicrucians began appearing all over Protestant Germany.

Michael Maier may also have been responsible for planting the seeds of Rosicrucianism in England. Details of his proselytizing efforts there are difficult to ascertain, but it is known that in 1615 Maier went to England on a diplomatic mission. And in that same year Robert Fludd of London became a convert to Rosicrucianism. Like Maier, Fludd was a physician of the Paracelsian school. He would eventually establish himself as one of the seventeenth century's most eminent philosophical alchemists.

Born in 1574, Robert Fludd was the child of an affluent minister who was greatly favored by Queen Elizabeth. The son attended Saint John's College, Oxford, where he proved to be a serious student with broad interests that ranged from languages and music to astrology and medieval history. He was also a pious young man—perhaps even a bit of a prude. He wrote disparagingly of students who "consorted with women," and he believed that sexual desire was the principal cause of humanity's original fall from grace.

Alchemists packed much symbolic information into pictures like this one, based on the following terse instruction: "Make a circle out of a man and woman, derive from it a square, and from the square a triangle: make a circle and you will have the philosopher's stone." Such drawings, said one adept, "depict with sufficient clarity for clairvoyant eyes what is most secret and hidden in the Great Work."

Fludd prided himself on having remained a perfectly "unstained virgin."

After receiving a master of arts degree at Oxford in 1598, he traveled for six years on the Continent, intent on broadening his education. During this period, Fludd was attracted equally by metaphysics, alchemy, natural history, theology, physics, and medicine. He sought the company of distinguished scholars in many disciplines and apparently absorbed a great deal of knowledge from these teachers. Not the least of his accomplishments was becoming intimately acquainted with the writings of Paracelsus, whose views on chemical medicines and alchemical philosophy struck the young man as original and exciting. Fludd's sexual attitudes aside, he was by nature something of a freethinker, and he had in the course of his travels grown more and more inclined to turn his back on the traditional teachings of both medicine and philosophy.

At the age of thirty-one, he returned to England, his mind awash with untested theories on medicine and chemistry. He obtained a medical degree at Christ Church, in the process ruffling the feathers of many of his instructors, who were still committed to the teachings of the second-century Greek physician Galen. Because of his controversial views, Fludd required more than four years to win the status of fellow in the College of Physicians. Once he had achieved that standing, however, he set up a thriving practice in London.

The medical care that Fludd provided was praised even by physicians who disagreed with his philosophy. His approach encompassed science as well as mystical healing—with a healthy dose of astrology thrown into the mix. He also relied on common sense and an appealing bedside manner. According to one contemporary, the doctor "spoke to his patients amusing them with I know not what, till by his elevated expressions he operated them into a faith-natural, which consequently contributed to the well working of the physic."

Lamentably, Fludd's voluminous writings on medical subjects dwell mainly on mystical theory and contain few examples of specific treatments. It is known that he placed great stock in analyzing the color of his patients' urine; in one of his medical tracts, he devoted nearly 200 pages to this form of diagnosis. Red colors, for example, he took as a sign of excesses in the digestion; pale colors, on the other

The Precarious Life of a King's Goldmaker

Johann F. Böttger promised to make gold.

In the autumn of 1701, a German newspaper carried a report of Johann Friedrich Böttger, a sixteen-year-old "pharmaceutical assistant who a few weeks ago transformed several 20-pfennig pieces into good gold in the presence of a number of aristocratic persons in Berlin." Böttger's employer assisted by melting the silver coins and noted that by adding "some tincture, which was of dark red glass," Böttger "instantly made" the silver into "finest gold which passed all examinations."

The uproar brought Böttger to the notice of such thinkers as Gottfried Wilhelm Leibniz, who wrote that he hesitated "to believe all I hear, and yet I dare not contradict so many witnesses." But Böttger also attracted Friedrich I of Prussia, whose passionate craving for gold led him to execute the alchemists who disappointed him.

Böttger elected to flee to a neighboring province rather than be pressed into Friedrich's service. Yet he became a captive "goldmaker" to a no less greedy king, Augustus the Strong of Saxony. The young man was installed in the well-equipped alchemical laboratory of the king's "gold house," where he could perform every possible investigation. But Böttger was never free to leave, and he well knew the fate of failed goldmakers—death on a gallows mockingly decked with tinsel. Through eighteen years in Augustus's employ, Böttger kept the king convinced that he could make gold and silver. He wrote many pledges and signed many contracts with the king, promising anything to save his skin.

Böttger did produce riches for the whole province, but not through transmutation. Trade with China had taught Europe the delights of porcelain. Whether in the form of fine tableware or exquisite statuary, this startling white, translucent material was more durable and more delicate than any European earthenware. No one had managed to imitate porcelain, and in 1706 the king commanded Böttger to find out how to make it.

Within three years the alchemist devised a manufacturing method. In 1710, Augustus had a porcelain factory built in Meissen, the first of many such world-famous German facilities. Böttger oversaw the factory for most of his remaining years, and the secret of porcelain-making came to be almost as guarded as that of the philosopher's tincture.

Despite Böttger's triumph, the king's hunger for riches grew. In the spring of 1713, Augustus demanded a demonstration of Böttger's powers of transmutation. On March 20, in a long metallurgical process conducted before the king and his closest advisers, Böttger appeared to meet the demand. Beginning with copper and lead, he somehow created a dollop of gold and of silver. He was saved from execution, but not from further demands.

In December 1717, Böttger swore he would soon give the king his goldmaking formula. But the alchemist's death, apparently from the effects of working with noxious substances, intervened, and his secrets died with him.

These two buttonlike "reguli," one nearly pure gold and the other nearly pure silver, were cast by Böttger in his famous alchemical demonstration for Augustus the Strong of Saxony on March 20, 1713. A witness reported that Böttger made these precious metals "from lead and copper with one grain of tincture." At first carefully preserved in the kingdom's secret depository, these pieces of "chemical" gold and silver are exhibited now in the Dresden Porcelain Museum.

In the letter at left, Böttger swears "before God and the Holy Trinity" to give Augustus of Saxony the "arcanum," or secret of the alchemical process. In the document below, the king vows to free his captive and promises to "never, in no place and at no time" compel Böttger to stay in his lands. Some of their many contracts were thirty-two pages.

hand—like those of white beans or cabbage stalks—indicated overheating.

In addition to tending his thriving medical practice, the energetic Fludd found time to indulge many other interests. His writings include more than a dozen works on subjects ranging from arithmetic to music and military science. Another favorite pastime was designing and building whimsical machinery for use in the masques and other popular stage entertainments of his day. One of Fludd's contraptions included a wooden ox that bellowed and threatened to charge, while a mechanical dragon hissed and spat flames in return.

Whatever other interests occupied his time, Fludd's special passion was always reserved for alchemy, and he expounded at length on the topic in a two-volume history of the microcosm and the macrocosm. He read widely in occult literature and corresponded busily with like-minded scholars in England and on the Continent. When he was exposed to the doctrines of the Rosy Cross Brotherhood, he was won over to the cause immediately. Particularly striking to him was the Rosicrucian emphasis on the oneness of all natural things. Like Khunrath and many of the mystical alchemists, Fludd was a devout Christian, and he was particularly struck by the Rosicrucian precept that the highest human goal was to know God.

Putting aside his other writing projects, he published a strongly worded tract in which he embraced the philosopy of the Rosicrucians and declared himself eager to join the brotherhood—if they chose to have him. There is no evidence, of course, that he ever became more than a supporter in principle of the fraternity. Indeed, his later writings would seem to suggest that he came to regard the brotherhood as strictly a symbolic creation.

Fludd's commitment to the Paracelsian concept of understanding the macrocosm by studying the microcosm kept him somewhat apart from the tradition of practical alchemy. He was definitely not one of Severinus's band of stout-shoed truth seekers. Instead, Fludd viewed alchemy as an elite vocation that called him to "worke uppon the invisible parts of man only with the eys of contemplation." Laboratory work with fire and bellows he denigrated as vulgar and trivial.

Yet Fludd realized that not everyone could grasp the essential truths of nature purely by means of philosophical example. For the benefit of less meditative students of alchemy he described an experiment he had devised to discover "the spirit of wheat." In the laboratory, he subjected kernels of the grain to the processes of heating, smoking, cooling, and steeping, until he had produced a slimy, smelly, dark residue, which he designated as the "first matter." Falling back on the time-honored medium of fire, Fludd then distilled the residue once, twice, and eventually five times, until he had extracted what he considered to be the "quintessence" of wheat.

According to Fludd's account of the incident, a remarkable thing occurred when his wheat experiment was nearly complete. By chance, he left a vessel containing some of the quintessence beneath a leaky section of the roof, and it partially filled with rainwater. A few days later he found the jar swarming "with wormes of a strang shape, . . . very long, slender and passing white." Fludd concurred with alchemical tradition in believing that rainwater was perfectly pure, and he was certain that the jar had been empty and clean before he added the quintessence. He concluded, therefore, that the worms could have arrived only through spontaneous generation—that they were the product of the "the vitall nature" residing in wheat.

Because of his advocacy of the great work, Fludd was frequently embroiled in controversies with other physicians, theologians, and philosophers in England and abroad. One of his most contentious debates erupted in the early 1600s

English physician Robert Fludd practiced medicine with an alchemical bent and published his elaborate theories in several beautifully illustrated books. The 1617 engraving at right, rich in alchemical symbolism, shows his idea of creation's plan and owes much to Rosicrucian lore. God reaches out from a radiant cloud to hold the chain that binds Nature, the "soul of the world." Nature holds a chain attached to the physical world, represented by a monkey. Humans, women, plants, animals, the arts, the elements, and the planets have their assigned places; the outermost rings are Paradise.

Integræ Naturæ
ſpeculum, Artisque imago
Elementum
Aquæ et Terræ.
Homo.
Aurum
Argentum
Mulier.
Plumbum.
Cupri
Leo.
uva.
Aquila.
Anguis.
Limax
Delphin.
Pisces.
Ars naturam corrigens in regno minerali.
Ars naturam adjuvans in regno vegetabili.
Ars naturam Supplens in regno animali.
Artes Liberaliores.
Mineralia.
Vegetabilia.
Animalia.
Elementum Aeris
Elementum Ignis.
Sphæræ Lunæ
Sphæra Mercurij.
Sphæra Veneris
Sphæræ Solis.
Sphæræ Martis
Sphæra Iouis.
Sphæra Saturni
Cælum Stellatum.

and concerned a rather bizarre medical treatment known as weapon-salve therapy. This alchemical remedy was extolled by the Paracelsians and disparaged by almost everyone else. It was applied in cases of wounds inflicted in battle and involved the use of a magical ointment that smacked strongly of witchcraft. Arguments for and against this treatment flared up on both sides of the English Channel for a substantial part of the seventeenth century—and Fludd was a leading English proponent of the therapy.

A recipe for the healing ointment was supposedly passed down from Paracelsus. It included two ounces of moss taken from a buried skull, half an ounce of embalmed human flesh, two ounces of human fat, two drams of linseed oil, and one ounce each of oil of roses and bole armoniack—the last being a kind of acidic earth. To this aromatic mixture the physician added a little blood taken from the patient. When the wound had been cleansed, the salve was applied and the injured limb was bound with bandages that had been dipped in the patient's urine.

Few of Fludd's contemporaries found anything curious or objectionable about the treatment up to this point. It was the last step that provoked argument: The Paracelsians believed that the salve should also be applied to the weapon that had caused the injury—only then could the ointment do its healing work. By a mystical process of animal magnetism, the salve on the sword would act on the wound, drawing on the sympathetic "life spirit" that was presumed to flow between them.

The treatment seemed reasonable to Fludd, for it evoked what he considered to be a long-established principle of curing by sympathetic action—in this case, the sympathy between the blood that stained the weapon and the blood that remained in the patient's body. In Fludd's own words, "the cure is done by the magnetique power of this Salve, caused by the Starres, which by the mediation of the ayre, is carried and adjoyned to the Wound." The dispute over the validity of this course of treatment was never resolved to the satisfaction of all, but the salve gradually disappeared from common use.

As a physician, Fludd was acutely interested in the subject of blood. He attended lectures given by the great English anatomist William Harvey, whose careful observations had shown for the first time how blood circulates through the body. It was typical of Fludd's general outlook on the world that he supported Harvey's conclusions not because he was impressed by the experimental evidence but because he found it logical to assume that blood should circulate—after all, the heavenly bodies do the same as they move through the macrocosmic sphere.

Many of Fludd's peers called him to task for such circuitous reasoning, but never to the point of questioning his standing as one of the seventeenth century's leading intellectuals. Fludd remained throughout his life a highly respected physician and savant; he also became an esteemed musician and a well-liked citizen of London. He died, unmarried, in 1637 and is buried in Bearsted Church near Maidstone, England. A fittingly bookish statue of the scholar at his desk marks his final transmutation.

The mysticism of Fludd's philosophy was countered by the somewhat more practical focus of a Belgian contemporary named Jan Baptista van Helmont. Born in 1577 to a noble family, Helmont studied and practiced medicine. But he became so absorbed by what seemed to him the limitless possibilities for applying chemistry to the care of the sick that he retired to his castle near Brussels to devote himself to research and experimentation. For most of his life, Helmont left the grounds of his stronghold home only when necessary to attend to his patients, and he never asked payment for his treatments. By the time of his death in 1644, he was renowned throughout Europe for his good works and learned writings.

Helmont is remembered today as a pioneer whose discoveries contributed in important ways to the modernization of medicine and chemistry. He was, for instance, the first anatomist to recognize the physiological functions of the stomach and to understand the digestive process. On the chemistry front, he was one of the earliest investigators to perceive that gases have distinct identities, as opposed to being mere varieties of air. It was Helmont, in fact, who popularized the use of the word *gas* in its current sense, having expropriated the Dutch word for effervescence. He is also credited with the discovery of carbon dioxide, which he referred to as "gas sylvestre."

These contributions now belong to the realm of science, but they were made in the name of alchemy. Like Severinus, Helmont had a reverence for the great work and paid homage to the alchemical furnace. He wrote that philosophers would never be "admitted to the Root, or radical knowledge of natural things, without the fire." Moreover, he made no secret of his belief in the reality of phenomena such as transmutation, the elixir of life, and the philosophers' stone. The last of these concepts particularly fired his imagination. While Helmont did not claim to understand how the stone worked, he insisted that he had witnessed its effects on several occasions, "even as Books do Promise."

Helmont's search for the prime constituent of life—another age-old preoccupation of alchemists—combined rigorous hands-on investigation with mystical leaps of faith. He rejected the Paracelsian *tria prima*—mercury, sulfur, and salt—and was unconvinced by the earth-air-fire-and-water explanation of Aristotle. In their place he adopted an even more ancient teaching to the effect that all things were derived from water. In what came to be known as his willow-tree experiment, Helmont monitored the growth of a willow shoot in a soil-filled pot. He demonstrated his respect for scientific quantification—a preoccupation unknown in earlier eras—as he carefully weighed the shoot and the soil before planting his tree. He noted that the willow weighed exactly 5 pounds and that the soil, when dry, weighed precisely 200 pounds.

For the next five years he watered the tree faithfully, and when it had grown to a substantial size he had it uprooted and then repeated the measurements. He found that the willow had gained 164 pounds, while the soil had lost a negligible two ounces. To Helmont this clearly demonstrated that "all Vegetables do materially arise wholly out of the Element of water." Understanding little about the processes by which plants grow, he had wrongly inferred that they were created from water, since they required moisture to survive.

As a philosopher, Helmont was committed to the notion of universal causes, and he jumped to an even broader false inference on the basis of the willow experiment. He decided that if water was the *prima materia* for plants, it must also be the starting point for animals, minerals, and anything else that might exist on the planet. To his way of thinking, this theory would explain a wide range of puzzling phenomena. It would account for the presence of chemicals in waters at spas and would explain how minerals found their way into the veins that marked the crust of the earth. The mineral deposits he attributed to the "stonyfying juyce" of flowing streams.

Helmont's published works were widely read on both sides of the English Channel, and one of the people most impressed by his theories was another leading figure in the

Jan Baptista van Helmont, a physician and wealthy nobleman, found his early studies of medical authorities "altogether fruitless" and so devoted himself to chemical experiments.

The Quest for a Perpetual-Motion Machine

While most alchemists tried to transmute base metals into noble ones, a surprising number were nearly as fascinated by another elusive goal: perpetual motion. As the name implies, a perpetual-motion device would run forever without requiring any additional expenditure of energy.

Robert Fludd and Robert Boyle were among the noted alchemists who tried to achieve this ideal. But the majority of proposed solutions were conceived by lesser-known inventors, and most never left the drawing board. Four such sketches appear on these pages.

Many designs were based on the notion of an overbalanced wheel, in which moving weights would keep one side heavier than the other. Other designs hoped to exploit the natural properties of water, air, and magnetism. A few perpetual-motion machines were built, and some seemed to work for a while. But in every case, they slowed to a halt or were exposed as frauds. The idea was doomed—except in one important respect.

Like the quest for transmutation, the pursuit of perpetual motion contributed valuable knowledge to science. During the 1800s, scientists reached an understanding of the laws of thermodynamics. These principles make clear that perpetual motion is an impossibility. They dictate that energy cannot be created or destroyed, only converted from one form to another, and that it can never be harnessed with perfect efficiency by any machine.

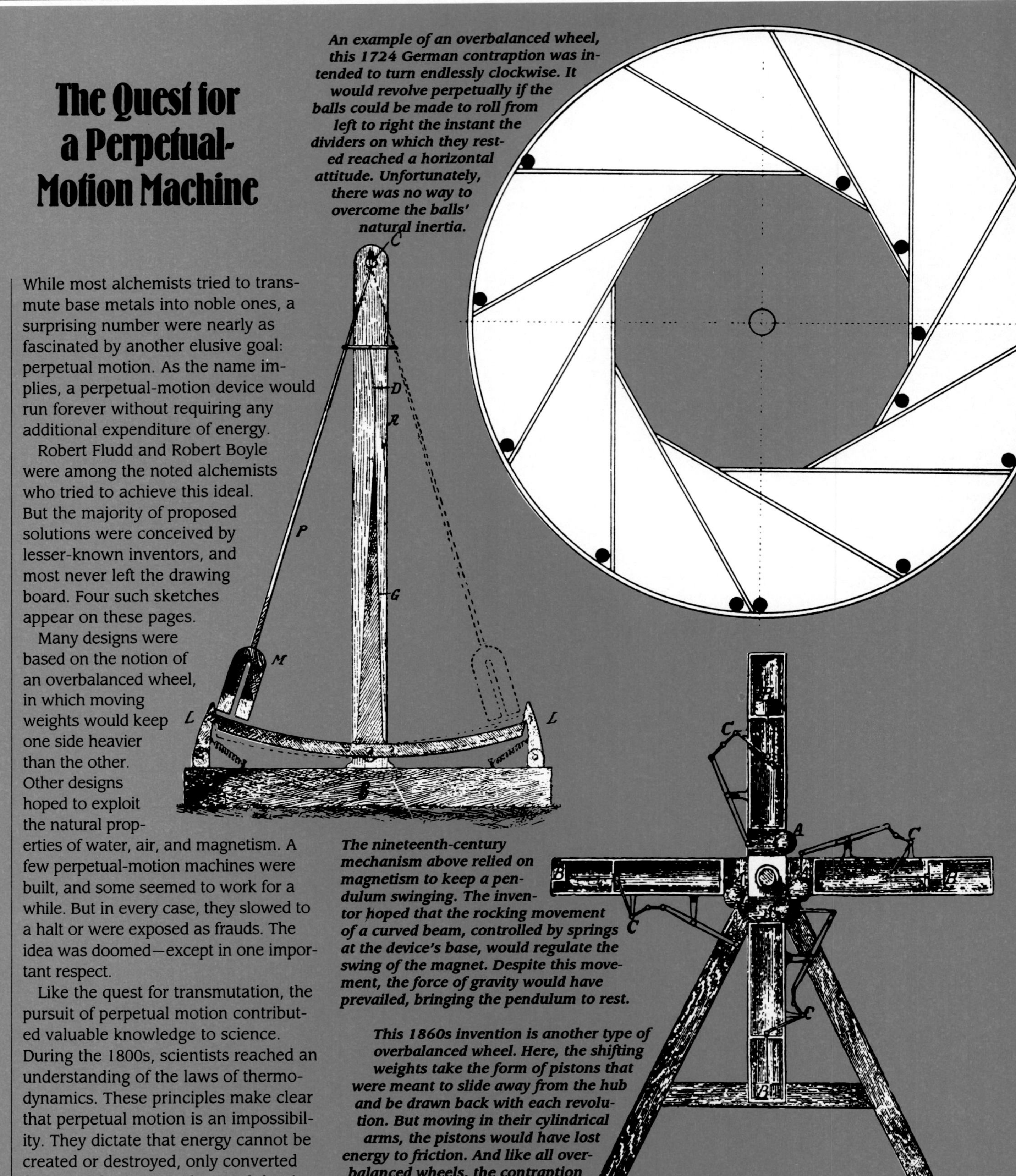

An example of an overbalanced wheel, this 1724 German contraption was intended to turn endlessly clockwise. It would revolve perpetually if the balls could be made to roll from left to right the instant the dividers on which they rested reached a horizontal attitude. Unfortunately, there was no way to overcome the balls' natural inertia.

The nineteenth-century mechanism above relied on magnetism to keep a pendulum swinging. The inventor hoped that the rocking movement of a curved beam, controlled by springs at the device's base, would regulate the swing of the magnet. Despite this movement, the force of gravity would have prevailed, bringing the pendulum to rest.

This 1860s invention is another type of overbalanced wheel. Here, the shifting weights take the form of pistons that were meant to slide away from the hub and be drawn back with each revolution. But moving in their cylindrical arms, the pistons would have lost energy to friction. And like all overbalanced wheels, the contraption would have succumbed to its overall equilibrium.

An 1865 Swiss design called a buoyancy motor relied on a revolving chain of floats. In theory, the air-filled balls would be buoyed up through the water in the chamber on the right. But the inventor failed to suggest a way to bring the balls in without letting the water escape.

new generation of experimental scientists. British physicist Robert Boyle was the fourteenth child of the earl of Cork, born in Ireland's Lismore Castle. He attended Eton and then traveled extensively before settling in England to undertake a life of study and scientific research.

A man of seemingly limitless interests, Boyle devoted himself particularly to physics and chemistry. He is probably best remembered for the scientific principle he extrapolated by observing that the volume of a gas is inversely proportional to the pressure to which it is exposed. Over his lifetime, Boyle explored a host of other natural phenomena, including sound waves, the refractive powers of crystals, the chemistry of combustion and of respiration, and the expansive force of freezing water. Apparently, however, he shied away from most investigations of biology, because a certain "tenderness of nature" inhibited him from making anatomical dissections.

An intellectual heir to Francis Bacon, and to the Rosicrucians as well, Boyle was something of an oddity in alchemical circles because he believed in sharing all the knowledge he gained through his research in any field. This put him at odds with the majority of adepts, who guarded their secrets fiercely. Boyle allied himself with a group of intellectuals known as the Invisible College, and he was a prominent member a decade later when the organization became the Royal Society of London for Improving Natural Knowledge. This was the same group that, more than a century later, unwittingly hounded James Price to his death.

As a practicing chemist, Boyle was attracted to Helmont's cosmological view that water was the one essential element in living organisms. He accepted the willow-tree experiment as unimpeachable evidence that his forerunner had been correct. But Boyle did not go along with Helmont's corollary that water gave rise to inorganic materials as well. He wrote that the Belgian scientist had provided "no instance of the production of minerals out of water" and insisted that, until he had seen explicit proof that water could generate minerals, he could not take such a theory seriously.

Yet when it came to the transmutation of metals, Boyle was a believer to the core. In a paper submitted to the Royal Society in 1676, he described years of experimentation with a specially refined form of mercury that he claimed had unique transmuting properties. It seems that Boyle never arrived at any particularly satisfactory conclusion to his alchemical ventures, but all his life he remained committed to the idea of transmuting gold. His optimism about the enterprise led him to lobby for the repeal of a statute against "multiplying gold" that had been on the books since the time of King Henry IV. He was successful at least in that effort.

Boyle also arrived at thought-provoking results through his chemical experiments in pursuit of the prime constituent of life. He concluded that there was no single substance at the heart of all matter but many distinct "corpuscles." In *The Sceptical Chymist,* his first book on chemistry, published in 1661, Boyle wrote: "I now mean by Elements . . . certain Primitive and simple, or perfectly unmingled bodies; which not being made of any other bodies, or of one another, are the Ingredients of which all those call'd perfectly mixt Bodies are immediately compounded, and into which they are ultimately resolved." This explanation is not all that far removed from the modern understanding of elements distinguished by their specific atomic structures. Scientist and alchemist to the end, Boyle died in 1691.

Another of Helmont's intellectual heirs who strove to combine alchemy and experimental science was an American-born physician named George Starkey. An avid Hermeticist from early in his life, Starkey studied medicine at Harvard in the 1640s and practiced it briefly in Boston, while carrying on extensive alchemical experiments in search of "a secure way of curing Diseases." Concluding that Boston was an intellectual backwater, he emigrated in 1650 to London, where alchemy was enjoying a flurry of speculative interest thanks in large part to the influence of Robert Boyle.

Starkey soon found his way into Boyle's Invisible College, where his colleagues were initially much impressed by their American adept. He revealed to the Invisibles several manuscripts on alchemical subjects that he claimed had been given to him by another American alchemist, Eirenaeus Philatheles. The authorship of the Philatheles manuscripts has never been firmly established, but most scholars are of the opinion that George Starkey wrote the books himself. What is certain is that he collaborated with physicist Robert Boyle in devising a chemical formulation that met with extensive praise as a remedy for fevers, sweating, rickets, and vomiting.

The American's welcome in London eventually wore thin, however, because of his tendency to promise more than he could deliver and his haphazard record for paying the bills of his suppliers. Starkey was also apparently of fragile mental health, prone to falling into deep depressions when he failed to attain his goals. One of his peers compared him to "a good vessel with much saile and little ballast." At some point, Starkey fell hopelessly behind on the expenses he had incurred buying chemicals, furnaces, glass bottles, and the like. His home was seized and he was sent to a debtor's prison. But the experience proved not all that disastrous, for he was allowed to continue his experiments in his cell.

When Starkey emerged from prison, he set even more sail than before, publishing in 1657 an attack on the Royal College of Medicine and the attitudes of its graduates. The work was called *Nature's Explication and Helmont's Vindication: Being a Short and Sure Way to a Long Life.* In it, he declared that the prevailing attitudes of physicians were mired in Galenic backwardness, despite the token innovations of adopting a few chemical treatments. He ridiculed most of the popular medicines of the day as "nonsensical, fortuitous prescripts," designed only to line the pockets of the doctors and the owners of apothecaries. This challenge won him no more support in his profession than would a similar critique today.

Starkey's last years were ever more contentious, and even his death in 1665 would provoke controversy. In that

Robert Boyle saw chemistry as a discipline in its own right, apart from alchemy or medicine. In his most famous work, The Sceptical Chymist (below), he challenged 2,000-year-old beliefs about the world's elements, noting that his ideas came not from the study of philosophers "but from the nature of things and from Chymical experiments themselves."

THE
SCEPTICAL CHYMIST:
OR
CHYMICO-PHYSICAL
Doubts & Paradoxes,
Touching the
SPAGYRIST'S PRINCIPLES
Commonly call'd
HYPOSTATICAL;
As they are wont to be Propos'd and
Defended by the Generality of
ALCHYMISTS.
Whereunto is præmis'd Part of another Discourse
relating to the same Subject.

BY
The Honourable *ROBERT BOYLE*, Esq;

LONDON,
Printed by *J. Cadwell* for *J. Crooke*, and are to be
Sold at the *Ship* in St. *Paul's* Church-Yard.
MDCLXI.

year there was a devastating outbreak of bubonic plague, and Starkey took up the verbal cudgel against the many doctors who were taking flight from London's noxious precincts. With a fellow chemist-physician named George Thomson, he ridiculed the Galenists for their cowardice and lack of understanding of the epidemic. Starkey insisted that, contrary to prevailing view, the disease had nothing to do with the cyclic influences of heavenly bodies. It had its seat in an internal illness, which enlightened physicians should be able to treat with the proper chemical medicines.

Thomson and Starkey challenged the London medical community to join them in dissecting an infected corpse so that they might come to a better understanding of the deadly illness. Unhappily, Starkey himself succumbed to the plague shortly after having administered chemical medicines to the ailing Thomson. The latter recovered—probably owing no thanks to the medicines—to perform the dissection alone. Starkey's enemies then circulated the false story that he had collaborated on the autopsy and had died along with a number of his colleagues within minutes of opening the pestilential corpse.

Watching from the sidelines during the plague year of 1665 was a twenty-three-year-old genius named Isaac Newton. One of the greatest scientific minds of his or any other generation, Isaac Newton is still revered for his spectacular contributions to modern physics, astronomy, and mathematics, including the discovery of the laws of gravitation and the invention of calculus. There is clear evidence, however, that—like so many of the dominant thinkers of his time—Newton also had a deep interest in alchemy and was a sometime practitioner.

In fact, Newton is said to have read more widely in alchemical literature than perhaps anyone before him. He accumulated an extensive library of 175 basic texts, conducted many experiments, and wrote numerous commentaries on the theories of other alchemists. Significantly, not one of the papers was published in his lifetime.

Newton embraced alchemy because he hoped that in the mystical secrets of the Hermetic arts he might find the underlying truths of natural philosophy and of the true religion that "God had imparted . . . to a select few." He believed that divine wisdom had been lost long ago in the biblical past but had been partially recovered by wise men like Hermes Trismegistus, "at which time it was incorporated in fables and mythic formulations where it would remain hidden from the vulgar."

Newton's letters reveal that he kept in close touch with other scholars engaged in alchemy, swapping formulas, ingredients, and apparatus. Just four years after completing his landmark work, *Philosophiae Naturalis Principia Mathematica,* he wrote to his friend John Locke about the latter's intention to replicate one of Robert Boyle's alchemical experiments. In a letter dated July 7, 1692, Newton complained that he had no way of carrying out the test on his own, because he had somehow dropped from his pocket parts of Boyle's recipe for the procedure.

For all his enthusiasm, Newton's experiments were no more successful than Boyle's had been. He never published any of the results or even made overt reference to the work in print. As a respected academic and—in his later years—warden of the royal mint, he may have thought it imprudent to make public his avocation, for alchemy was already beginning to lose some of its luster in England.

In fact, succeeding generations of scientists influenced by Isaac Newton were reluctant to even acknowledge their master's interest in the subject. Not until 1936, when the great man's descendants offered at auction a collection of his private papers, did the depth of Newton's commitment to alchemy become widely known.

The famous and elusive Saint-Germain convinced many European aristocrats he could create gold. On his death, a royal benefactor destroyed his papers, lest they be misconstrued by the ignorant. His epitaph reads, "He who called himself the Count de Saint-Germain and Welldone, of whom there is no other information, has been buried in this Church."

While luminous alchemists and scientists such as Fludd, Helmont, Boyle, and Newton were pursuing Hermetic studies in the seclusion of their libraries and laboratories, the average citizens of the period were much more aware of the everyday variety of would-be adepts, who moved among them offering everything from spiritual enlightenment to material wealth. These practitioners were nearly as numerous in Newton's age as they had been in the time of Paracelsus. They usually claimed to possess the dual powers of extending life and changing dross into gold. Some were legitimate healers and true mystics, but most were out-and-out mountebanks, and the gold they extracted came mainly from the pockets of the gullible.

So rife was the seventeenth century with alchemical fraud that Gabriel Plattes, an English gentleman and science buff, was provoked to publish in 1655 a pamphlet of warning called *A Caveat for Alchymists.* It was designed to help "Gentlemen that studieth this Art" identify the true alchemist and avoid the "smoak seller," who might persuade them to enter into ill-considered and costly investments.

Some sixty years later, Lady Mary Wortley Montagu, an inveterate letter writer and social commentator, noted the continuing popularity of alchemy on the Continent with a disapproving eye. Writing to her daughter in 1717, she

In 1677, when alchemist Johann Wenzel Seyler von Reinburg presented this engraved plate to Leopold I (whose likeness is at the center), it was dull gray rather than shining gold. But then, before the emperor and his court, the self-proclaimed goldmaker lowered the sixteen-pound plate into nitric acid, which ate away the coating of gray metal and thus "transmuted" the plate to gold. Such tricks were common among the many fraudulent alchemists of the day.

The man who called himself Count Cagliostro was a flamboyant clairvoyant, faith healer, and fortuneteller, but he met with less success in alchemy. In one demonstration, a Polish courtier caught him slipping a nugget of gold into a crucible of base metals. "Cagliostro," declared a knowledgeable Frenchwoman, "has been driven out of every country in which he has tried to make gold."

reported, "There is indeed a prodigious number of alchymists at Vienna" and added that a "pestilential passion" for chemistry had already ruined several noble families. She also confided in her daughter that "even the Emperor is supposed to be no enemy to this folly in secret, though he has pretended to discourage it in public."

By Lady Mary's time, the "smoak sellers," or puffers, were generally skilled chemists who knew very well how to mask their tricks so as to escape detection. A French chemist known as Geoffrey the Elder provided an eye-opening catalog of their deceptive techniques: "They often used double-bottomed crucibles or cupels, lining the bottom with oxides of gold or silver, then covering it with an appropriate paste. They also sometimes made a hole in a lump of coal and poured gold or silver powder in it; or sometimes they soaked coals with solutions of these metals, then pulverized them before projecting them on the substances to be transmuted. . . . They stirred fused substances with wands or little wooden batons; these had been hollowed out at one end, filled with gold or silver filings, and then stopped up again. . . . Small grains or tiny ingots of gold and silver were hidden inside lead, and reappeared when the lead was calcined in a cupel."

One of the most persuasive and charismatic of the alchemists who may have resorted to such tricks was the comte de Saint-Germain, also one of the celebrated mystics of history. Where Saint-Germain came from or who he really was probably never will be known, for he was a master of disguise and impersonation. He passed himself off at various times as Italian, Polish, Spanish, Russian, Hungarian, and German; he always carried an impressive title and was fluent in the language of the moment. The year of his birth is also unclear, and given that he never seemed to grow any older, some of his contemporaries were convinced that he was—as he claimed—hundreds of years old. Most historians, however, believe that Saint-Germain was probably in his early thirties in 1743 when author Horace Walpole mentioned the presence in London of a spy, priest, fiddler, and "vast nobleman."

That same year the countess d'Adhemar, a confidante of the French queen Marie Antoinette, reported that "a foreigner, enormously rich, judging by the magnificence of his jewelry, has just arrived at Versailles." As always, Saint-Germain's origins were impossible to pin down, but the countess marveled at his knowledge of the world and concluded that he was better acquainted with the foreign courts than were any of the king's ambassadors. Even the skeptical Voltaire was dazzled and referred to Saint-Germain as "a man who never dies, and who knows everything."

Others commented on the mystery man's gifts of clairvoyance and telepathy, his beautiful singing voice, his excellence as a violinist and composer, his perfect ambidexterity, and his astonishing ability to recall every word of a text after a single reading. Not even his dietary habits escaped unnoticed. By all accounts, Saint-Germain observed a high-fiber, low-cholesterol diet—a concept unknown at the time—consisting of oatmeal, groats, and the white meat of chicken, even at the otherwise sumptuous royal table.

Nothing, however, matched Saint-Germain's acclaim as a practical alchemist. The amorous Italian adventurer Giovanni Casanova grudgingly admitted that, in this regard at least, Saint-Germain had won his admiration. In his memoirs, Casanova described crossing paths with the adept in a town near Brussels and prevailing upon him to show off his transmuting agent, which was called *athoeter.* As the Italian described the encounter, "It was a white liquid contained in a well stopped phial. He told me that this liquid was the universal spirit of Nature and that if the wax of the stopper was pricked even so slightly, the whole of the contents would disappear. I begged him to make the experiment. He thereupon gave me the phial and the pin and I myself pricked the wax, when, lo, the phial was empty." Casanova inquired what practical purpose such a phenomenon might serve, but Saint-Germain would say only that it was a secret.

Saint-Germain was also said to possess the power to change flawed and common stones into gems of incalculable value. He claimed to have acquired this skill in India, and indeed, he gave away gems with such liberality that many of those around him believed he produced the stones through alchemy. Saint-Germain once had a difficult moment in Amsterdam, however, when the authenticity of his jewelry was questioned, and he was forced to decamp abruptly in order to avoid arrest.

He eventually ran afoul of French law as well, when he dabbled in foreign diplomacy. He was accused of treason but then was allowed to circumvent prosecution simply by leaving the country. Saint-Germain had no difficulty finding a new home; he settled in German Schleswig, where a wealthy landowner called Charles of Hesse gave him the wherewithal to pursue the occult arts in private. He lived out his life under Charles's benign protection and died, by most accounts, in 1784. Yet reports of reappearances by the mystic would spring up in various European cities for several decades thereafter.

Saint-Germain is still a genuinely mysterious figure. Although he was extravagantly admired in his lifetime—and never seriously prosecuted by any authority—most historians now regard him as purely an opportunistic poseur. Some modern spiritualists, however, see him in a different light. To this day, Saint-Germain is proudly claimed as a member in good standing by certain Masonic and Rosicrucian orders. He is even revered by a few spiritual sects as a living saintly presence.

Before Saint-Germain departed the earth, he seems to have taught a trick or two to another controversial personage, the notorious Count Cagliostro. As was the case with Saint-Germain, most details of Cagliostro's history are subject to debate. But his exploits attracted lavish attention while he was alive, and his story has inspired historians, novelists, playwrights, and composers for nearly 200 years since he died. The various accounts of his life disagree dramatically on numerous specifics, but the tale is never dull.

Most historians identify Cagliostro with Joseph Balsamo, a rather rough-and-tumble Sicilian born in 1743. Young Balsamo studied chemistry as a novitiate in a monastery, where he was sent for a dose of discipline after several adolescent escapades. He was soon put to work in a pharmacy and showed a considerable gift with flask and flame. But his temperament was clearly not suited to monastic life, and he eventually left, moving to Palermo, where he took up a career in skulduggery.

After stealing sixty ounces of gold, Balsamo fled to Messina, on the eastern tip of Sicily. There he changed his name to Alessandro Cagliostro and, for good measure, added the title of count. For a short while, he traveled the eastern Mediterranean in a rather peripatetic search for arcane knowledge and magical powers. But soon he settled in Rome, where he married a woman named Lorenza Feliciani, who came from a good family and provided him with a handsome dowry.

Some accounts suggest that Cagliostro forced his wife to sell sexual favors in order to augment his income. Whether that story is true or not, he somehow fell out with his father-in-law and the Roman authorities. He and Lorenza abandoned Rome for a life as itinerant magicians. Not until Cagliostro adopted the role of alchemist, however, did fortune come his way. In the late months of 1772, when he was perhaps no more than twenty-nine years old, Cagliostro and his contessa were settled in Paris and living—as usual—precariously. One night, he dressed in a spectacular costume and appeared at an elegant ball where he knew the cream of society would be gathered. After making his entrance, Cagliostro grandly announced that he had mastered the great arcanum of the philosophers' stone. The simple ploy worked to perfection, and soon offers of patronage were arriving from all sides.

Within a year, Cagliostro and Lorenza had accumulated a fortune of some 100,000 crowns, most of it handed over by a foolish Portuguese nobleman in exchange for nothing but promises. Moving on, the couple visited the celebrated Saint-Germain at his domicile in Schleswig. They hoped for a glimpse of yet another sort of arcane performance art—and Saint-Germain did not disappoint them.

According to the so-called *Authentic Memoires of Cagliostro,* he and his wife received extensive instruction in mystical practices and the rituals of magic. Cagliostro claimed that Saint-Germain taught them never to tell the truth. The Sicilian passed on the advice accordingly: "Do not foolishly regulate your actions according to the rules of common sense; rather outrage reason and courageously maintain every unbelievable absurdity."

Whatever Cagliostro's fraudulent failings, it seems clear that he had a working knowledge of chemical medicine, and some people believe that he may have been possessed of certain psychic or telepathic powers as well. One way or another, he acquired a remarkable reputation as a healer and mesmerist. Wealthy favor seekers came to him in droves, showering him with gifts and begging to be initiated into the Masonic lodges that he and Lorenza established. In St. Petersburg, Catherine the Great was impressed by Cagliostro's powers, and in German Strasbourg, the cardinal prince de Rohan gave up much of his wealth to the persuasive pair, who promptly decided to return to France and the court of Louis XVI. In France, ironically, Cagliostro and his wife were implicated in a crime they did not commit—a complex swindle involving a fabulous diamond necklace. They were eventually exonerated, but their luck ran out when they moved back to Rome and made the mistake of trying to establish a Masonic temple in the very shadow of the Vatican.

Arrested on charges of heresy in September 1789, they were sentenced to life imprisonment, after a lengthy trial. Lorenza is believed to have perished in 1794 in a women's penitentiary. Cagliostro died the next year, after six years of solitary confinement in an underground dungeon. Legend holds that arcane symbols covered the walls of his cell, and the possibility exists that Cagliostro hoped until the very end to effect a sort of magical rescue by finding the philosophers' stone at last.

No one can doubt that within a few years of Cagliostro's death the golden age of alchemy was over. Even though they were practicing alchemists themselves, scientific pioneers like Robert Boyle and Isaac Newton had begun to bring down the curtain a full century earlier. Yet their work had little immediate impact on European culture at large, and there was no clear-cut moment when alchemy lost its grip on the popular imagination. Indeed, considering the lively attention brought into focus by Saint-Germain, Cagliostro, James Price, and the other self-proclaimed adepts of the eighteenth century, it was clear that the allure of the great work would linger long after its sun had set.

The Great Work in the Orient

As much as a thousand years before the first European alchemists plied their mystical craft, another form of the ancient art was well established in China. Chinese alchemy was widely practiced at least as early as the second century BC—and perhaps long before then. It flourished in one form or another until the 1700s and has not completely died out even in contemporary times.

Like its Western counterpart, Chinese alchemy mingled spiritual aspirations with pragmatic physical techniques. But while European alchemists focused primarily on the transmutation of base metals into gold, Chinese alchemists single-mindedly pursued a more lasting reward: immortality.

According to Chinese adepts, eternal life could be achieved by several different methods, including those explained on the following pages. The alchemists took a practical view of immortality, considering it simply the result of extremely good health. In fact, many of the measures they prescribed were similar to the recommendations endorsed by modern Western medicine: physical exercise, mental conditioning, and a moderate diet.

Other approaches were neither as accessible nor, in hindsight, as sensible. Certain Chinese alchemists sought eternal life in exotic diets that included items like pine nuts and cranes' eggs. Some concocted and drank elixirs containing gold, silver, and other expensive—and sometimes poisonous—minerals; adepts often made attempts to manufacture these ingredients themselves to save money.

To the more spiritually inclined alchemists, however, the mechanics of goldmaking and healthful living were only external symbols of a deeper reality suggested in the diagram seen here. In this picture, the adept brings order to the world around him, represented by paired animals symbolizing the complementary universal opposites yin and yang, as well as by the Chinese ideograms for fire, water, wood, metal, and earth. The elixir that results from the adept's work appears at the base of the diagram as a cascade of orderly streams. Such a fountain "induces harmony and immortality in everything it flows over," a modern authority on the art of Chinese alchemy explains. "That is the virtue of the elixir, but it is also the power of the sage."

A rootlike version of the human spine stretches from bottom to top in this nineteenth-century diagram of the body's inner cosmos. Qi is said to flow along the spine from its base near the sexual organs (depicted here by fire), through a tranquil midsection (denoted by farming and spinning), up to a reservoir in the head.

Bearded philosophers examine a symbol of yin and yang in this detail from a seventeenth-century silk scroll. Within the divided circle they study, black represents yin (the feminine principle associated with the earth, passivity, and darkness); white represents yang (the masculine principle linked to heaven, activity, and light). Since each depends upon the other, the yin region includes a white embryo of yang, and in a like manner, the yang region holds a black embryo of yin.

The vital force qi flows from heaven into the body of the adept in the abstract diagram below, whose meaning was once revealed only to alchemy's initiates. Such drawings could be carried for personal protection, or they could be burned and the ashes eaten as a way to restore lost youth.

A Cosmos Energized by Yin, Yang, and Qi

From the fourth to the first century BC, Chinese thinkers developed a basic philosophical picture of the universe that would undergo little change for more than a millennium. Accepted by early alchemists, these ideas had a lasting influence on the fledgling craft.

According to this classic world-view, everything in human experience consists of *ch'i,* or *qi,* a cosmic essence symbolized in the serpentine diagram at left. Qi is a totally pervasive phenomenon: It not only causes all change, it also comprises the matter that undergoes change. In the body, qi serves as the vital energy that makes life possible, as illustrated in the representation of a human spine at left above. Improving the circulation of qi through the body can bring health or immortality; obstructing its flow can cause illness or death.

Qi has two complementary aspects: yin and yang. Although yin is sometimes associated with death and yang with life, both are present in the human body and thus are part of the alchemical process. Only by bringing them into balance could an adept open the door to eternal life.

The Inner Alchemy of Mind and Body

Perhaps the most straightforward Chinese route to immortality was the so-called inner alchemy of mental and physical exercise. Through this rigorous conditioning, it was hoped that an adept could be so purified and strengthened that his mind and body would never fail.

Deep, controlled breathing was an essential foundation of inner alchemy, since air and breath were identified with the vital essence qi. Techniques of breath control could be almost alarmingly vigorous, as in the version described by one early observer. "Huffing and puffing, breathing out and breathing in, blowing out the old qi and drawing in the new, hanging like a bear, and stretching like a bird," the witness wrote, "all this merely shows the desire for long life."

More restrained breathing strategies called for exhalation so gentle that it would not ruffle a wild goose feather held before the nose. Such quiet respiration was then combined with meditation on images like the ones pictured below, intended to instill the clear, calm vision of a true immortal.

To avoid the dangers of a wholly sedentary lifestyle, the ancient Chinese alchemists also performed what can be described as a kind of ritual gymnastics. In 1973, archaeologists examining a tomb from the second century BC discovered a rare, painted silk record of dozens of these exercises, most accompanied by explanations that define their physical or spiritual purpose. Six of the figures, hand-copied from the badly fragmented original, appear at right.

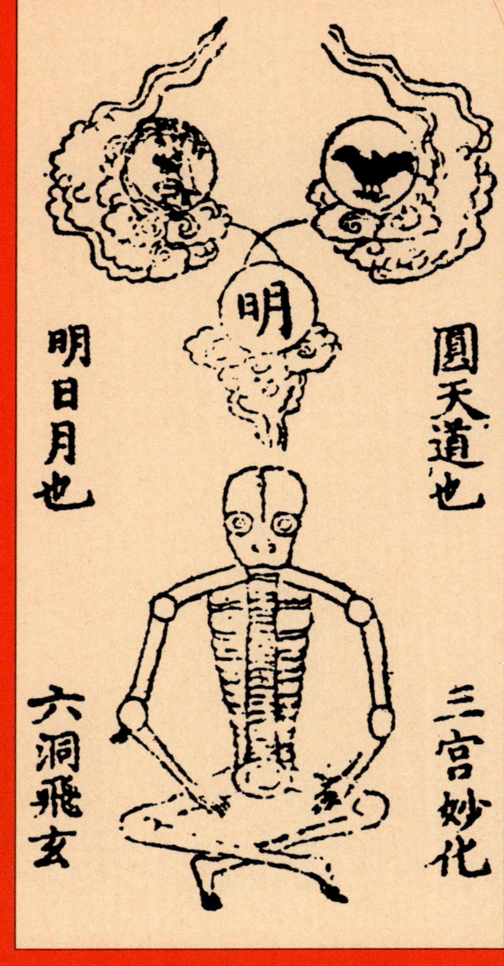

In this fifteenth-century aid to meditation, the pictured alchemist metaphorically reduces himself to a skeleton, shedding the sensations of the flesh to focus on enlightenment of the mind. Above his head, the ideogram for illumination draws together the principles of yin and yang, represented respectively in this scene by a roughly sketched rabbit on the moon (upper left) and a three-legged raven on the sun (upper right).

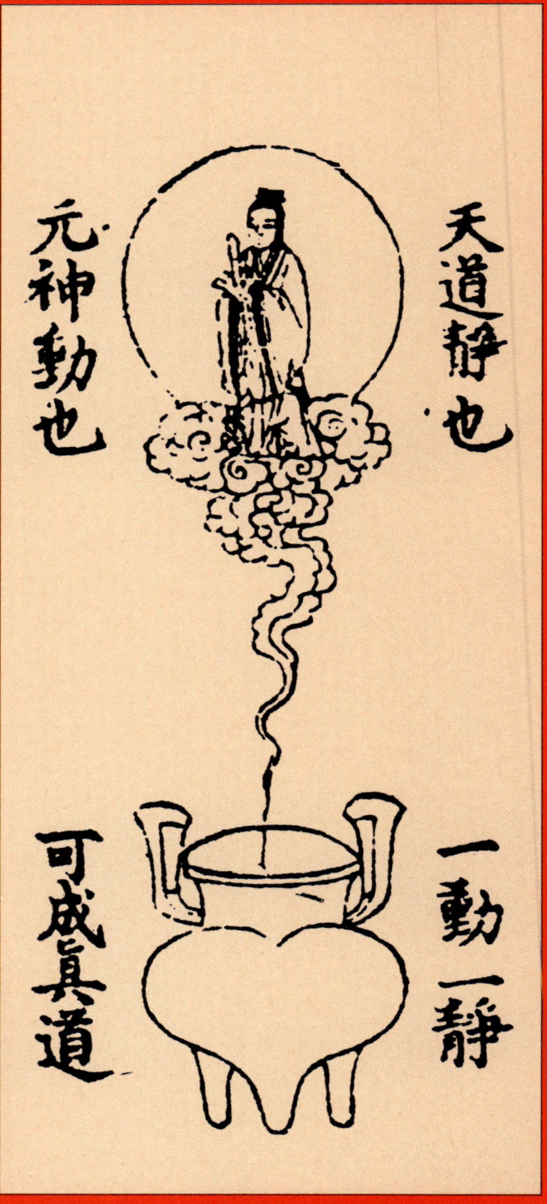

Fumes from a vessel heated on the alchemist's furnace waft him toward immortality in another fifteenth-century meditation drawing. Furnaces had spiritual as well as physical significance for the ancient Chinese, some of whom were said to have worshiped a domestic god of the stove.

A limber adept takes up the praying-mantis position in one of several exercises from a silk painting buried in 168 BC.

The alchemist stretches legs, arms, and back in a yogalike pose that was called "head down, pushing upward."

Reaching one hand toward heaven and the other toward the earth, the adept "joins yin and yang with a staff."

This vigorous sideways extension known as the sparrow hawk was among the more demanding ritual stretches.

The adept imitates an archer drawing a bow in this exercise for the chest and arms.

An exuberant gesture dubbed "looking up and exhaling" combines a back stretch with careful breath control.

Drawing Vital Energy from the Natural World

"If you desire to keep your body youthful forever," wrote a third-century authority, "do not eat fat or rich food; use salt and spices with moderation." Following that common-sense advice, most Chinese adepts ate lightly and fasted often. Some also consumed a curious dietary supplement: the flesh and fiber of long-lived animals and plants, which were thought to owe their longevity to an abundance of qi.

Because cranes were believed to live a thousand years, their eggs became an ingredient in alchemical recipes. Similarly, the ground-up shells of aged tortoises figured in the diet of certain adepts, and tortoise soup was considered highly invigorating.

In the realm of plants, nuts from a kind of long-lived pine tree were thought to confer immunity from heat, cold, hunger, thirst, and ultimately death itself. Ordinary peaches were considered powerful, but not so potent as a variety called the peaches of immortality. These were said to grow in the legendary island garden of the queen of the immortals; a single bite brought life everlasting.

Such animals and plants were considered so effective, in fact, that it was not always thought necessary to eat them. Simply being near images like those shown here was supposed to vastly increase one's chances of eternal life.

The tortoise, seen confronting a writhing serpent in this eighth-century rendering, was traditionally associated with immortality because of its longevity.

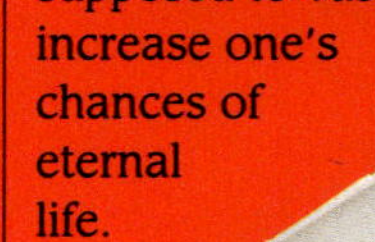

A celestial dragon guards the pearl of human and cosmic energy in this detail from a nineteenth-century emperor's silk robe. Because dragons were thought to be extremely long-lived, if not immortal, robes embroidered with their likenesses were said to bring good fortune and long life to the lucky wearer.

Two young women take their ease in a family garden depicted on this eighteenth-century plate bordered by the cranes of immortality. Near the women, an outgrowth of pink peonies represents wealth and nobility; above them, the flying yellow feng bird—a Chinese version of the phoenix—embodies the idea of spiritual rebirth. Those who dined from a plate with such auspicious animal and plant associations were believed to greatly enhance their chances of immortality.

Mystical Powers of the Mineral Kingdom

If meditating, exercising, and eating plain food ever proved too wearisome, the alchemy of ancient China offered yet another approach: the laboratory synthesis of immortality elixirs. Derived from rare or costly ingredients, these magical pills often included cinnabar, a red crystal of mercuric sulfide. Some incorporated gold, silver, or jade—a material also thought to protect the dead from decay *(far right).* Outside the laboratory, these precious minerals were used to create lucky objects like those below and at right.

Swallowing mineral elixirs could be hazardous *(see box, below right).* It was also expensive. To cut costs and control the purity of their materials, alchemists tried making gold and other metals themselves, typically by speeding up processes thought to create the substances in nature. But the prospect of cheap gold proved an open invitation to fraud and greed. By the 1200s, goldmakers had so little credibility that reputable alchemists turned permanently to the internal, meditative forms of the art.

Auspicious animal and plant images ornament the back of a silver and bronze "cosmic mirror" from the Tang dynasty. Mirrors were highly valued in ancient China, not just for their rarity, but because they reflected the owner's soul.

Although few objects were made entirely of cinnabar, alchemists could readily acquire household items coated with a cinnabar-based lacquer, like the modern box above. Owning such objects was thought to promote good health, longevity, and ultimately immortality.

Classic but Dangerous Remedies

The ultimate goal of laboratory alchemy in China was the elixir of immortality, a crystalline pill equal in importance to the philosophers' stone in the West. Ironically, however, such alchemical remedies could bring sudden death rather than eternal life. According to Chinese records, a number of alchemists—and several emperors—succumbed to fatal doses of the mystical substances. Often the cause was mercury poisoning, since many alchemical recipes called for ingredients of pure mercury or mercuric compounds.

In spite of the attendant danger, immortality elixirs and similar but less potent medicines still seemed to offer enough hope to the prospective user that they remained popular well into the tenth century. For example, one recipe that appeared in the seventh-century text *Tan ching yao chuch* (Essential Formulas from the Alchemical Classics), directed the alchemist to form pills about the size of large "hempseeds" from a mixture of jujube paste, powdered rhinoceros horn, musk, cinnabar, sublimated sulfur, and mercury. Among the ailments that were supposedly eased by this potentially deadly combination were anxiety, nervous palpitations, indigestion, stiffness, poor eyesight, deafness, contagious fever, symptoms said to be brought about by unseasonably hot winds, dropsy, poisoning, heart attack, and even demonic possession.

Lying in state on an ornately carved headrest, the burial suit of Han prince Liu Sheng incorporates 2,690 pieces of jade, drilled at the corners and sewn together with golden wire. Thought to offer immortality to the living, jade was also supposed to preserve the bodies of the dead. But archaeologists who unearthed the 2,200-year-old suit found no trace of Liu, who had long since turned to dust.

Entering the Realm of the Immortals

Believing in so many opportunities to achieve eternal life, Chinese alchemists were convinced that at least some of their number actually had become *xian,* or immortals. What happened after that depended on the individual xian. Some lived on the fringes of society, exerting a benign influence on human affairs. Others chose to meditate in mountain caves. Still other xian were thought to have ascended to the Realm of the Immortals, a misty never-never land depicted below and at right.

Chinese tradition also honored the Eight Immortals *(far right).* Highly individual in their looks and habits, these xian rank among the most popular figures in Chinese folklore.

High in the Realm of the Immortals, cloudborne spirits carrying lanterns, brooms, and parasols approach a rocky plateau associated with yang.

Against a dreamlike backdrop of mountain peaks and clouds, scholarly immortals welcome a new arrival to their realm on this eleventh-century hand scroll.

Zhongli Quan

Before he became immortal, this potbellied warrior commanded an unsuccessful military expedition against Tibet. Fleeing in disgrace after his defeat, he encountered Master Donghua, a venerable alchemist who taught him the secret of eternal life. Zhongli Quan later went on to confer immortality on Lü Dongbin (right).

Lü Dongbin

Despite his position as a patron saint of literature, Lü Dongbin invariably carried a two-edged sword, the hilt of which can be seen here just behind his left shoulder. This weapon was not intended for ordinary combat, as Lü once explained: "It is ridiculous to believe that an Immortal kills. I possess a sword, but it is used for different purposes: extirpating avarice, passion, and vexation."

He Xiangu

The only woman among the Eight Immortals, demure He Xiangu was noted for her modesty and sense of duty. She acquired immortality at the age of thirteen after a seemingly accidental encounter with Lü Dongbin (left), who was dressed as a priest. Because she showed great respect, he gave her one of the peaches of immortality.

Cao Guojiu

Depicted here idly tossing a pair of castanets, Cao Guojiu began life as the brother of a queen. As he traveled through China, the young man carried a medal showing he had the emperor's protection. One day a priest scolded him for relying on influential connections, and Cao threw the medal into a river. The priest—actually Lü Dongbin—then inducted him into the Eight Immortals.

Han Xiangzi

The great-nephew of a prominent philosopher, Han Xiangzi once wrote an alchemical poem for his great-uncle that made reference to melted pearls and magical fungi. "Show me the man who does these things in the way that I have told," concludes the verse, "and I will gladly talk with him of the xian who ne'er grow old."

Li Tieguai

This member of the Eight Immortals once left his body for seven days, only to discover on his return that it had been cremated. He quickly occupied the nearby corpse of a recently deceased beggar, where he then remained. Named for the iron crutch, or tie guai, on which he leaned, Li Tieguai manifested his true identity in the swirling smoke that rose continuously from the gourd he carried.

Zhang Gualao

A historical figure of the Tang dynasty, Zhang Gualao was also the subject of several legends concerning his later existence as an immortal. According to one story, he rode a mule that could cover thousands of miles a day, yet could be folded like a piece of paper each night. To revive his mount the next morning, the sage squirted it with a mouthful of water.

Lan Caihe

This popular vagabond was a lively drunk famous for his witty repartee. In more serious moments, he sang songs of immortality that gained a wide following. "Our real hope is up in the clouds," went one line. "There you'll find tall palaces of silver and gold." True to his word, Lan Caihe vanished one day into the sky on a crane, leaving behind his clothing, a boot, and a pair of castanets.

CHAPTER 4

The Alchemists of Today

he last thing on most Americans' minds in 1941 was alchemy. Even devoted Hermeticists were caught up in the global preoccupations of World War II, which increasingly threatened to involve the United States. But in the summer of that year, three scientists—Rubby Sherr, Kenneth T. Bainbridge, and Herbert H. Anderson—accomplished what generations of alchemists had dreamed of: They performed the "great work."

In the subdued environs of a Harvard University laboratory, the team bombarded some 400 grams of mercury with a blizzard of high-velocity neutrons and then placed the irradiated sample in a vacuum distilling flask. Amid the molecular debris they found three isotopes of gold. Granted, the amount of the precious metal was minute. But unlike every previous attempt over the long history of Hermetic aspirations, this transmutation was genuine beyond the shadow of a doubt. The Harvard scientists had conducted their experiment in a thoroughly controlled environment; the results were indisputable. In language a world away from traditional alchemical lore, the team reported their findings: "The products of the transmutation of mercury by fast (Li+D) neutrons were investigated. Three radioactive gold isotopes were found to be formed by the n-p reactions." That a base metal could be turned into gold was now a matter of scientific fact.

Some found it ironic that modern science, ever disdainful of alchemical pursuits, would ultimately substantiate the seekers' age-old beliefs. As early as the eighteenth century, science had been well on the way to consigning alchemy to the dusty attic of human thought. Fewer and fewer of the world's great thinkers seriously pondered what learned Arabs had once called the hidden science. By the late 1800s, scholar Hermann Kopp had branded alchemy "the history of an error." Around the turn of the twentieth century, however, some diligent chemists discovered that at least one of alchemy's fantastic claims—physical transmutation—was possible. They professed no alchemical inclinations or ambitions, though, insisting that this type of transmutation, which occurred at the subatomic level, would never be profitable. But their work eventually led to the successful experiment at Harvard in 1941—and rekindled the hopes of others, far removed from the scientific establishment, who still clung fast to the venerable aspirations of alchemy.

While breakthroughs in physics and chemistry rejuvenated physical alchemy, so the new science of psychology lent validity to the spiritual side of the so-called great work. As seminal a figure as Swiss psychoanalyst Carl Jung declared that alchemy's most noble ambitions were practically identical to those of the new breed of physicians who treated the inner mind.

Bolstered by the attention alchemy was receiving from such unexpected quarters, a modern-day generation of devotees embraced the work, and by many accounts they performed strange and wonderful feats, similar to the amazing deeds credited to their Renaissance forebears. And they found new ways to apply alchemical wisdom to contemporary concerns. Moreover, by the late twentieth century, theoretical physics had dismantled many scientific notions of the universe that earlier had seemed unassailable. To proponents of alchemy it began to look as if the old art's dismissal had been premature.

The theory of the atom proposed by John Dalton in the early nineteenth century and the theory of subatomic particles (protons, neutrons, and electrons) that emerged a century later could be construed as providing scientific terms for the ancient alchemical concept of *prima materia,* or primordial matter, the unifying substance from which all things and creatures derived. Furthermore, scientists began to speculate that if an atom's structure was somehow disrupted, it might change into the atom of another element. This theory was ratified by the discovery that radioactive elements can be *spontaneously* changed into different elements.

The first to observe these spontaneous transmutations were chemists Sir William Ramsay of Scotland and Frederick Soddy of England. In a carefully controlled laboratory investigation in July 1903, a spectroscope recorded fragments flying out of radium atoms, subtly but undeniably changing the atoms' original configurations into those of different elements.

But few elements are radioactive, and none spontaneously change into gold. Any alchemical ambitions might have ceased with Ramsay and Soddy if it had not been for Baron Ernest Rutherford, the British physicist who won the Nobel Prize in 1908 for his work on atomic structure. Rutherford wondered if the particles thrown off by radioactive substances might somehow be aimed at other elements to disrupt them intentionally.

He decided to use radium as his atomic cannon, since it shot out "bullets" of helium nuclei at 12,000 miles per hour. In one of a series of experiments, the physicist placed a small chunk of radium close to aluminum. The radium's barrage of helium particles knocked off pieces of the aluminum's atoms, which Rutherford identified as hydrogen. And the atoms that had originally been aluminum before some pieces were stricken off were simultaneously transformed into magnesium. Thus the aluminum had been transmuted into two other elements: hydrogen and magnesium.

There was nothing visually dramatic about the proc-

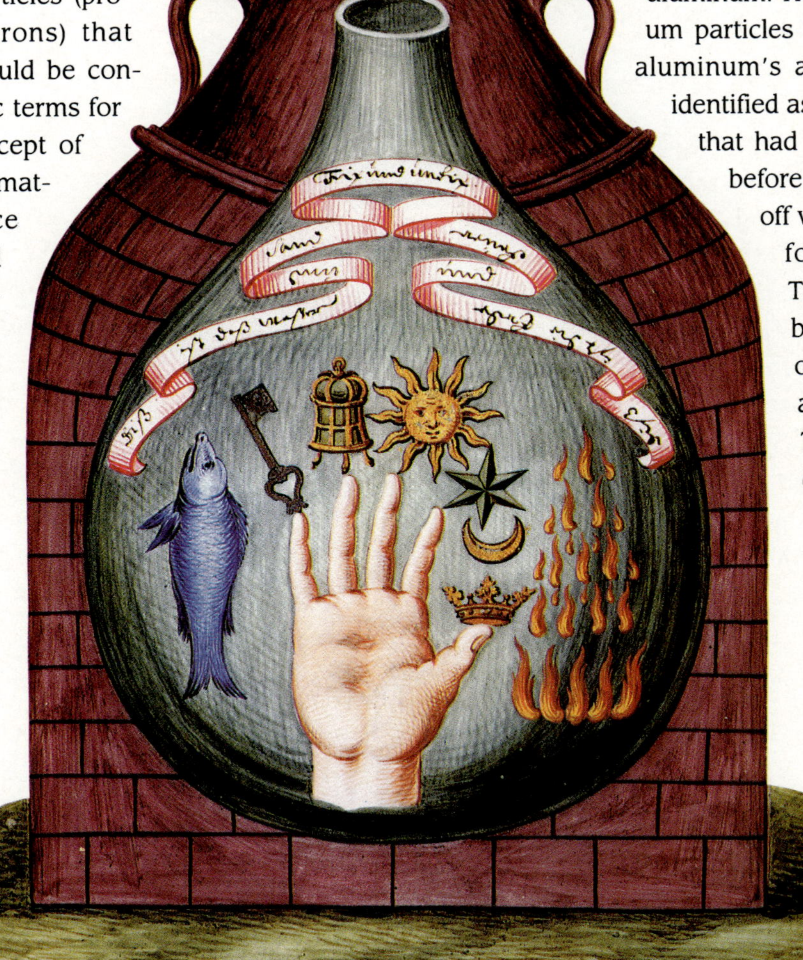

ess. "One can scarcely imagine a less striking experiment," observed one of Rutherford's contemporaries. "Only the trained eye can perceive it under the most favorable conditions." Nevertheless, Rutherford's experiments were the first deliberate—and demonstrable—transmutations of the scientific age.

These transmutations were on a scale unlikely to impress a latter-day Paracelsus, however. One scientist estimated that, using Rutherford's method, it would take a million years to create one cubic centimeter of hydrogen from aluminum; the amount of magnesium formed would be correspondingly small as well. In most cases, though, scientists were not concerned with the products of the transmutation or their amounts but with the behavior of matter and the energy released in such a reaction.

After a time physicists learned to predict what element would result in a transmutation by determining the number of particles subtracted from the original element. Each was found to have its own sum of atomic particles, and all elements were arranged according to their respective atomic weights on a scale that came to be called the periodic table of elements. Scientists determined that when protons in an atom's nucleus are removed, as occurred in the study conducted by Rutherford, the original element is transmuted into an element that is lower in atomic weight and occupies a lower position on the periodic table.

All this atomic arithmetic led to a renewed—sometimes feverish—interest in physical alchemy during the early twentieth century. Decades before Sherr, Bainbridge, and Anderson produced gold in their Harvard laboratory, a veritable rush was on to find a molecular recipe for the artificial creation of the precious metal. And at first, some conventional scientists untainted by the label of alchemist were in the thick of it.

The Curative Powers of a Noble Metal

Drinks with a trace of gold "make the heart happy," wrote sixteenth-century Hermeticist Paracelsus. Because alchemists associated gold with the sun, and the sun with the human heart, they prescribed gold-based medicines for ailments from chest pains to melancholy.

That practice may have inspired the sixteenth-century creators of Danziger Goldwasser, the liqueur pictured here. Still sold in Europe, "gold water from Danzig" contains flecks of 22-carat gold and a host of medicinal herbs. But although herbs and alcohol have undeniable effects on the body, the gold in Goldwasser probably does not. Doctors have known since the late 1600s that gold is all but inert and passes through the body unchanged.

Nonetheless, physicians have continued to try medicines based on gold compounds, substances in which gold is chemically combined with other elements. In the 1890s, Illinois doctor Leslie Keeley used double chloride of gold to treat tens of thousands of alcoholics at sanitariums throughout the United States. Grateful ex-patients founded clubs to popularize the Keeley cure, which did not survive the death of its inventor in 1900.

Another compound, gold cyanide, inhibits the growth of tuberculosis bacilli in a lab and became a common remedy for that disease in the early 1900s. Later clinical trials proved the treatment ineffective for people—but not before two French doctors tried gold compounds on patients suffering from rheumatoid arthritis.

The results of their work, published in 1929 and confirmed many times since, have offered substantial relief to arthritics. Although some show little response and a few suffer side effects, about 60 percent of those treated with gold compounds feel less pain, sleep better, experience fewer muscle cramps, and show measurable reductions in joint swelling, bone deterioration, and stiffness.

But despite its acceptance by the medical community, gold treatment is as mysterious today as in the age of Paracelsus. Until science learns the cause of arthritis, the way gold combats the disease will likely remain an enigma as well.

In 1924, a German physicist named Adolphe Meithe believed he had stumbled upon a method for synthesizing gold while studying the discoloration of minerals and glass by ultraviolet light. As he was examining a black soot that had formed on the mercury-vapor lamp in his laboratory, Meithe found that the deposit, which had caused the lamp to cease working, contained traces of gold. It is not unusual to find traces of gold in mercury, because mercury is one of the few liquids that will dissolve the precious metal, but Meithe was using mercury that was supposedly free of impurities. He hastily concluded, therefore, that the high-voltage electricity flowing through the lamp had disrupted atoms of the mercury, which sat at 201 on the atomic scale, dropping them down four places to the atomic weight of gold at 197. When Meithe went public with his findings, his announcement was quickly seconded by Professor Hantaro Nagaoka of Tokyo Imperial University, who claimed to have deliberately created gold through a similar process.

Meithe initially cautioned that the amounts of the precious metal in question were minuscule and that through this method gold would cost $2 million a pound to produce. A few months later, however, Meithe claimed to have improved his process 10,000-fold by bombarding mercury atoms with electrons in a vacuum. He received financial backing from a major German industrial firm, and rumors began to circulate that Germany was banking on Meithe's gold to pay off its staggering debts from World War I.

Others remained unimpressed, however. Challenging Meithe's claims, *Scientific American* magazine put up the money to enable New York University professor H. H. Sheldon to duplicate Meithe's experiment. Sheldon's equipment was more sophisticated than Meithe's, and he obtained his mercury from a source that was naturally free from gold. As *Scientific American* noted, "It does not appear that this particular precaution was observed by Professor Meithe." Sheldon failed to produce any gold at all. He concluded that Meithe's mercury, though twice distilled, had retained a few stubborn gold traces, which had merely been concentrated in the soot on his mercury lamp.

While Meithe's "transmutations" were being brought to earth, one of his countrymen, a former plumber named Franz Tausend, was approaching the apex of a spectacular if short-lived career as an "industrial" alchemist. Tausend had developed what he called a theory of "harmonic-periodics," in which every element had—in addition to its own atomic weight—a distinct frequency, like a musical note. Tausend claimed that by altering an element's composition and thus changing its frequency, he could create a new element. To prove his theory, he claimed to have devised a method for making morphine out of table salt.

In 1923, Tausend announced he had discovered a way to synthesize gold. He formed a research company, took out some newspaper ads, and in two years had managed to collect hundreds of thousands of deutsche marks in private funding. Tausend wooed his investors with convincing scientific jargon and rabble-rousing nationalism. As time passed, and his creditors grew anxious to see the fabulous returns he had promised, Tausend assuaged them with dramatic demonstrations of his methods.

Eventually, he teamed up with Gen. Erich Ludendorff, Hitler's right-hand man in the attempted overthrow of the Weimar Republic. Ludendorff was fund-raising for the Nazi party when he heard about Tausend's alleged miracles, and he decided to assemble a group of wealthy political allies to investigate the matter. Under strictly controlled conditions, Tausend melted quartz and iron oxide in an electric furnace, then added a sprinkle of white powder to this homemade lava. He let the crucible cool while his breathless audience waited; then, by all reports, Tausend smashed it open to reveal an ounce of pure gold.

On the spot, Ludendorff and Tausend established a concern called Company 164, and soon investment funds were pouring in to support further research. Within a year, Ludendorff managed to divert 400,000 marks into the Nazi party coffers, then abruptly quit the partnership. Tausend warded off nervous investors with a second demonstration on June 16, 1928, in which he was seen to make twenty-five

When Adolphe Meithe (above, left) claimed in 1924 that he had accidentally changed mercury to gold, the news made headlines worldwide. Hooded for protection against rays (like the experimenter pictured above), Meithe was using a mercury-vapor lamp (left) when he found minute deposits of gold on the lamp's rodlike electrode. An American magazine declared large-scale transmutation inevitable: "Financiers say that this would wreck the financial structure of the world. Very well. Let the financiers get ready. For artificial gold is one of the things that science is going to produce." But later experiments indicated Meithe's gold had existed all along as an impurity in the mercury.

ounces of gold in one shot. Again the money flowed, and Tausend retreated to his "research centers"—several villas and two castles he had acquired.

A year later, with nothing else to show for his efforts or his clients' investments, Tausend was arrested. At the end of a long and sensational trial—during which a few of his most loyal, or gullible, investors actually testified in his defense—he was convicted of fraud and sentenced to four years in jail.

Even then Tausend refused to give up. From his new home in a Munich prison, he somehow managed to persuade his guardians to take him to the state mint for one last demonstration. After being thoroughly searched, he was supplied with raw materials from the mint's carefully guarded safe. Then—in front of the state attorney, two detectives, and an examining judge—Tausend appeared to smelt one-tenth of a gram of the purest gold from one and a half grams of lead. His audience was dumbfounded—until the following morning, when the mint director found out that Tausend had managed to sneak the gold into the makeshift laboratory by concealing it inside a cigarette. He was promptly returned to jail, where he continued to maintain his innocence.

Nevertheless, Tausend's fate did not dampen the public's interest in what was being called scientific alchemy. As Tausend started to serve his sentence, a Polish engineer named Dunikowski threw Paris into an uproar with his purported method for transforming quartz into gold. Dunikowski said that his secret lay in exposing the mineral to "z-rays," a radiation supposedly even more powerful than x-rays. The self-avowed alchemist collected some two million francs in investments but failed to deliver the goods; like Tausend, he was imprisoned for fraud.

And, like Tausend, Dunikowski stubbornly persisted. After his release, he revealed to a group of scientists that his process did not *create* gold but instead *extracted* gold traces that naturally occur in quartz. Although this was a far cry from his initial claims, some powerful people were impressed. An Anglo-French consortium was developed around the Dunikowski approach, with an eye toward trucking in deserts worth of sand from northern Africa and extracting gold on a grand scale. Dunikowski disappeared at the outbreak of World War II; rumor had it that he was working secretly in a laboratory on the Swiss-French borderlands, making gold to finance the German occupation.

Keeping their eyes fixed on the bottom line, most physical alchemists of the early twentieth century seemed unconcerned with the ancient art's traditional spiritual and philosophical concerns. There was, however, one notable exception—at least ostensibly an exception. In 1926, a Parisian publisher named Jean Schemit printed a limited edition of a book entitled *Le Mystère des Cathédrales* (The Mystery of the Cathedrals). The author, identified by the single name Fulcanelli, wrote, "Behind the gargoyles and glyphs, the windows and the flying buttresses a mighty secret lay, all but openly displayed. . . . Wholly unsuspected by the profane, the Gothic cathedrals have for seven hundred years offered European man a course of instruction in his own possible evolution." In other words, the great secrets of alchemy had actually been built into the architecture of these enormous medieval churches.

Fulcanelli argued, for example, that the cruciform layout of medieval churches not only followed the lines of Christ's cross, but together with the apse (the rounded portion attached to the cross structure), it created the image of an ankh, which was the ancient Egyptian symbol for spirit encased in matter—a concept essential to alchemy down through the ages. Even the grand entrance to Notre Dame bore a powerful alchemical symbol: a carving of a female figure on a throne with her head in the clouds. The two books in her left hand—one open and one closed—represented to Fulcanelli the public and secret traditions of the Hermetic art, while a nine-runged ladder against her chest signified the nine stages of the great work.

The treatise was highly controversial among historians and clerics alike, but it was also clearly the work of a

Gen. Erich Ludendorff (left), who helped dupe investors in Franz Tausend's synthetic-gold scheme, poses with his friend Adolf Hitler. Hitler's Nazi party was to become a prime beneficiary of the scam.

brilliant mind with startling insight into all branches and ages of alchemy. The instant popularity of *Le Mystère des Cathédrales* was heightened by the mystery surrounding its author, who was nowhere to be found. A man identified as Fulcanelli's young protégé, Eugene Canseliet, wrote in the book's preface, "For a long time now the author of this book has not been among us. . . . Having reached the pinnacle of knowledge, could he refuse to obey the commands of Destiny? . . . Under the influence of that divine flame, the former man is entirely consumed." The implication of Canseliet's high-flown imagery was that Fulcanelli had achieved the final end of alchemy and had been raised beyond earthly existence to a higher realm.

Speculations abounded regarding Fulcanelli's identity and his fate. While some believed Canseliet's story, others surmised that Fulcanelli had gone into hiding to avoid being mobbed by alchemical enthusiasts. Still others thought that no such person existed, that Fulcanelli had been cooked up by Canseliet and other "disciples" as a way of promoting their Hermetic beliefs. The issue was further complicated by the book's illustrator, one Jean-Julien Champagne. A man who wore old-fashioned clothes and imbibed quantities of absinthe, Champagne was said to be the closest person to Fulcanelli and something of an adept himself. He had claimed success, along with Canseliet, in transmuting baser metals into gold.

In the 1930s, the publisher Schemit revealed that before he ever laid eyes on Fulcanelli's manuscript, he had received a visit from a "shortish man with a long moustache which swept across his cheeks in the 'Gallic' fashion." This stranger spoke about the connection between Gothic architecture and alchemy. A month later Canseliet arrived at Schemit's with this same man in tow and introduced him as Champagne. Schemit became convinced that Fulcanelli and Champagne were the same man. But neither Champagne nor Canseliet would corroborate his contention, and others found it unlikely for various reasons—such as, how could one as intemperate and indiscreet as Champagne write with the composed wisdom credited to Fulcanelli's work?

In 1937, five years after Champagne's death, a man calling himself Fulcanelli performed a remarkable demonstration at the Castle de Lere, near Bourges, France. Witnessed by two physicists, a geologist, and a chemist, he sprinkled "an unknown substance" into half a pound of molten lead. It allegedly changed to half a pound of gold as the four scientists looked on. Fulcanelli next proceeded to smelt 100 grams of silver and then supposedly transmuted it into uranium.

More than two decades later, an exiled Polish scientist and dabbler in the occult named Jacques Bergier claimed to have met Fulcanelli in that same year. In a book published in 1960, Bergier said he was in his laboratory at the Paris Gas Board in the summer of 1937, when his work was interrupted by the sudden appearance of a total stranger. The scientist said the stranger spoke in a "metallic, dignified

Franz Tausend, who claimed he could make "synthetic gold," stands in a German courtroom in 1931, charged with fraud. Trained as a plumber, Tausend presented himself as a doctor of chemistry and a baron, assuring investors he would manufacture the precious metal at a factory near Munich (below). After a colorful trial, during which it was said that even the Italian government had invested in the scheme, the judge called Tausend "a brazen and unscrupulous impostor." The sentence, however, was lenient, perhaps because Tausend apparently believed his own claims at the outset.

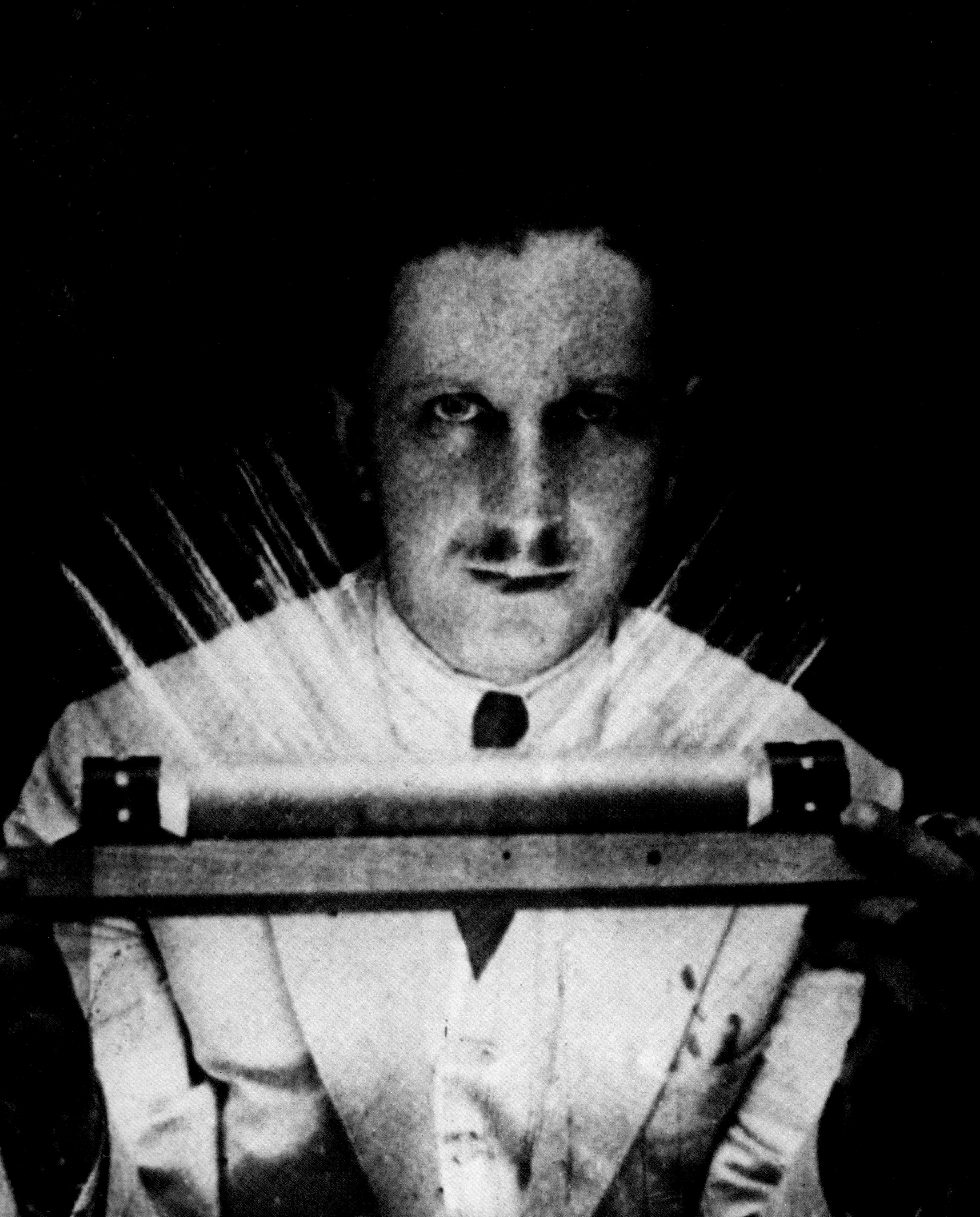

In a photograph retouched to include the radiating lines of so-called z-rays (left), Polish engineer Zbigniew Dunikowski gazes over a glowing tube, part of an apparatus he said could change sand into gold. His 1930 patent registration, accompanied by the diagram below, described a process in which sand was poured from a funnel (2) onto an electrified copper plate (1) and then was passed through an electrical field (3), radioactivity (4) "excited" by independent circuits (5), and ultraviolet light (6), to emerge as gold. He was later jailed for fraud.

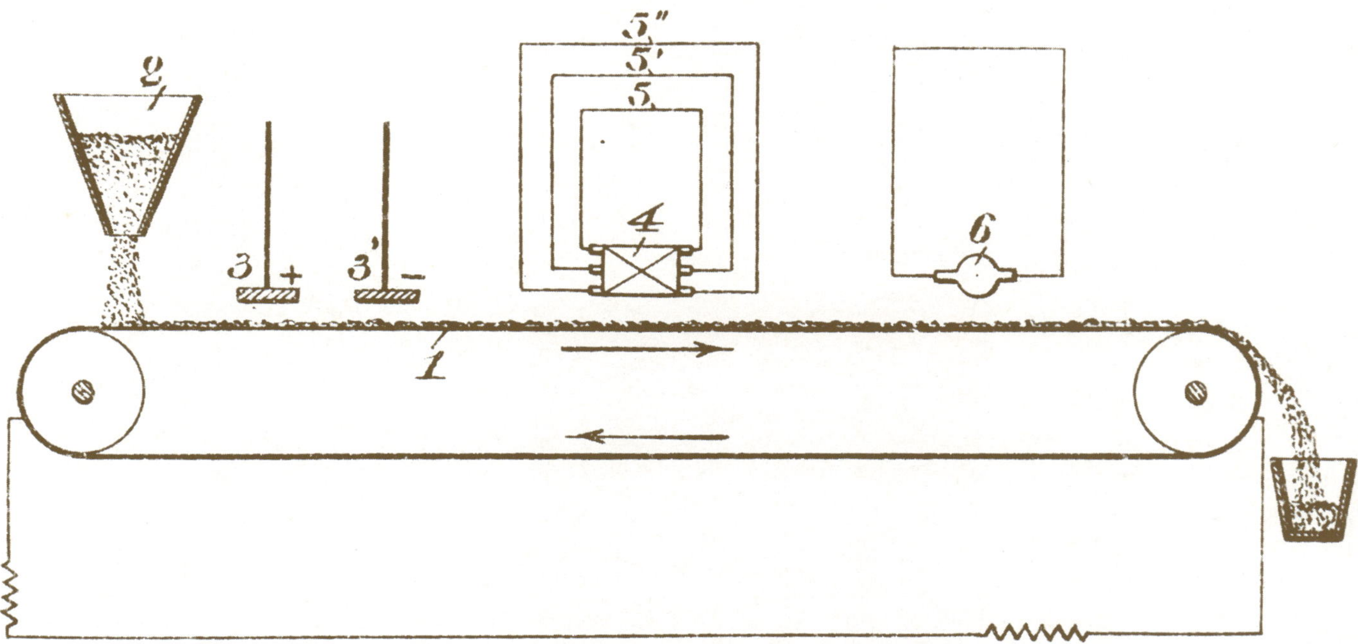

voice," calmly announcing that he knew Bergier was involved with experiments in nuclear energy. He also knew that Bergier's work focused on producing radioactivity with plutonium by electrifying a bismuth rod sunk in deuterium under high pressure.

"You are on the brink of success," declared the stranger, "as indeed are several other of our scientists today. May I be allowed to warn you to be careful? The work that you and your colleagues are undertaking is appallingly dangerous. It imperils not only you yourselves—it is a threat to the whole of humanity. . . . I am telling you this point blank: the alchemists have known it for a very long time."

Bergier related that he was shocked by this bizarre intrusion and prepared to counter with a modern-day, common-sense retort, but before he could utter the words the stranger declared: "I know what you are going to say, but it's of no interest to me. You think that the alchemists were ignorant of the structure of the nucleus . . . they have never achieved a transmutation, let alone released nuclear energy. I shall not try to prove to you what I now intend telling you, but . . . certain geometrical arrangements of highly purified substances are sufficient to release atomic forces without recourse to vacuum lines."

On the stunned Bergier's desk was a book by Frederick Soddy, Ramsay's partner in the discovery of spontaneous transmutation. The stranger picked it up, opened to a certain page, and read: " 'I believe that there were civilizations in the past that were familiar with atomic energy, and that by abusing it they were utterly destroyed.' "

He put the book down and looked hard at Bergier: "I ask you to believe that certain techniques have partially survived. I also ask you to remember that the alchemists have always taken religious and moral issues into consideration . . . while modern physics . . . is science without a conscience . . . I thought it my duty to warn a few research workers here and there, but I have no hope that my warnings will bear fruit."

Bergier said that although he never saw the man again, the weird interlude lodged in his memory. When he later read Fulcanelli's *Le Mystère des Cathédrales,* he was convinced that its author was the man he had met in the gas-works laboratory.

Bergier, it appears, was accused on several occasions of having participated in or staged occult hoaxes, and some believed that his story was a simple fabrication. And yet the Fulcanelli legend lived on. Years later, Eugene Canseliet claimed he had encountered Fulcanelli in Paris in 1952. At the time, Canseliet was fifty years old, which in normal circumstances would have meant that Fulcanelli was more than eighty. Canseliet insisted, however, that Fulcanelli appeared to be the same age as himself. To believe Canseliet was to believe that during his years out of public sight, Fulcanelli had been growing steadily younger.

Fulcanelli—whoever the man was—stood for the spiritual values inherent in physical alchemy. There is a whole body of modern alchemical thought that has ignored or discounted the physical great work, embracing alchemy exclusively for its spiritual rewards. This movement came to the fore in the nineteenth century, a period receptive to all manner of occult beliefs. The century spawned a number of impressive alchemical scholars, including Vermont-born Ethan Allen Hitchcock, grandson and namesake of the Revolutionary War hero and leader of the Green Mountain Boys of Vermont. Following in his grandfather's footsteps, Hitchcock led a long and distinguished military career through the Florida Indian wars, the Mexican-American War, and the Civil War, in which he served as President Lincoln's personal military adviser.

According to the French author known as Fulcanelli, alchemical secrets are preserved in the stonework of Gothic cathedrals like Notre Dame in Paris. The weather-beaten carving above, he suggested, depicts an adept defending his lab from interlopers.

In addition to being a fine soldier, Hitchcock was a highly literate man who devoured books voraciously. By 1853, Hitchcock had accumulated about 2,500 books, some of which explored the uncharted territories of mysticism. But it was not until a year later, in a New York bookshop, that he stumbled upon a crumbling volume on alchemy. He

To Fulcanelli's eye, the woman in this symbol-laden bas-relief was alchemy personified. He considered Notre Dame the architectural equivalent of the Mutus Liber, the famous wordless guide to the great work.

was hooked. After years of poring over every dusty tome he could find on the subject, he ended up writing a book of his own and published it in 1857. Entitled *Alchemy and the Alchemists,* the work proposed a revolutionary modern interpretation of the ancient Hermetic art, which nevertheless harked back to alchemy's origins.

Hitchcock's opening argument was that the transmutation of metals was never alchemy's true end but was instead a symbol of humanity's struggle toward spiritual salvation. As he wrote in the book's preface, the alchemist's "alembic, furnace, cucurbit, retort, philosophical egg, etc., etc., in which the work of fermentation, distillation, extraction of essences and spirits, and the preparation of salts is said to have taken place, was Man—yourself, friendly reader." Thus "the subject of alchemy was *Man;* while the *object* was the perfection of Man."

The rest of Hitchcock's book presented convincing evidence that all alchemical references stood for elements of the human soul. For example, mercury—the fluid metal that "yearned" toward gold—was a symbol of human consciousness, yearning for spiritual perfection.

If the goal of the great work was so straightforward, then why express it in obscure alchemical terms? Because, contended Hitchcock, alchemists, although they were strictly Christian, believed that people should become enlightened by self-discovery. This flew in the face of Church authorities, who thought "that coercion and violence might be legitimately employed to *force* men into the established public faith." So alchemists couched their subversive efforts in Hermetic jargon to avoid the hangman. According to Hitchcock, their efforts were only partially successful, for by saving "their own heads," they "plunged hundreds and thousands of the 'profane' into vain and useless efforts to find a *tangible* agent for turning the baser metals into gold."

Having been drawn to the subject by intellectual curiosity, Hitchcock seemed to have been converted to Hermetic philosophy as he studied the old masters. On November 12, 1866, he made this notation in his diary: "I wish to say that I saw, a moment since, what the Philosopher's Stone signifies. I have nowhere told what it is . . . but, when seen, has the effect something like looking into the sun. Personally I have much to fear from it, before I can look forward to its benefits."

Hitchcock probably did not know it, but just as he was formulating his theory on alchemy and humanity's quest for perfectibility, an anonymous author across the Atlantic was publishing a book whose thesis ran along the same lines. Appearing in London in 1850, *A Suggestive Inquiry into Hermetic Philosophy and Alchemy* proposed that alchemy was about regenerating the human soul. But the book went on to embrace what Hitchcock had rejected: namely, that as a secondary benefit, alchemy enabled honest practitioners to raise nonhuman entities, including metals, to their nobler condition. Physical alchemy was a natural by-product of spiritual alchemy, the author contended, but its misuse for material gain had betrayed the art.

The book went on to say that at the time of humanity's biblical fall, man also experienced an evolutionary fall. Only through supreme effort could people mature beyond the material world's plane to their true "unity and identity with the Universal Mind." According to *A Suggestive Inquiry,* spiritual evolution was not a matter of haphazard, divine intervention but was "an exact science" perfected by a few individuals in each generation. Through hypnotism, adepts could "magnetically unseal" their subjects and free their inner, divine light.

The story behind *A Suggestive Inquiry* is nearly as strange as the book itself. Its author turned out to be Mary Anne South, the thirty-three-year-old daughter of Thomas South, a gentleman of leisure who immersed himself in philosophy and metaphysics. Both father and daughter had read widely in alchemical texts, and both had experimented with hypnotism and psychic phenomena. The Souths believed that the scientific advances of their era were in fact the rediscovery of knowledge that alchemists had retained all along but had kept to themselves.

Thomas South had originally encouraged Mary Anne to publish *A Suggestive Inquiry* and actually paid for its printing. But soon after the book came out, he bought up all the outstanding copies, built a bonfire on the lawn, and burned the lot. A hundred copies had already been sold, however, and for years afterward Mary Anne bought them out of public circulation, one copy at a time, at premium prices. She later attributed the Souths' change of heart to moral panic. After the book was published, she and her father began to feel they had betrayed a "sacred secret" and had rushed to correct their error.

Mary Anne eventually wed a Yorkshire clergyman named Atwood and for the duration of their marriage forsook her interest in alchemy and other matters unseemly for a vicar's wife. Her husband died in 1883, however, and she lived on until 1910, when she died at ninety-eight years of age. Friends and admirers from her later years confirmed that Mary Anne South Atwood was a true intellectual—in an age when intellectual pursuits were still considered inappropriate for women in some circles. The fact that she was able to write her ill-fated book in such times was remarkable in itself, so much so that some have speculated that she must have had access to a mystical source of strength and understanding to have achieved it.

While many spiritual alchemists pursued their efforts in lonely obscurity, some of the most prominent intellectuals and artists of the turn of the twentieth century became deeply and publicly involved in Hermeticism. The most famous assembly of spiritual alchemists was the Golden Dawn, a semisecret order that included George Bernard Shaw's mistress, Florence Farr, and the great Irish poet William Butler Yeats.

The seeds of the Golden Dawn were sown in 1887, when Dr. William Wynn Westcott, a London coroner and a

The Healing Efforts of Contemporary Paracelsians

The healing and life-extending techniques touted by alchemists today run the gamut from the exceedingly bizarre to the comfortably practical. The two extremes are personified by British Hermeticist Swami Purna *(below, left)* and American Hans Nintzel *(below, right),* who were photographed together at a 1981 London party for occult magicians.

Purna, who claims to have graduated from Oxford University in 1845, attributes his supposed longevity to a tiny image of the Hindu god Shiva, which he carved from a block of solidified quicksilver and implanted in his flesh. The likeness, called a *gulika,* must be extracted and replaced every seven years.

By contrast, the elixirs cooked up by Hans Nintzel sound like grandmother's curative chicken soup. Typical is his tincture of rosemary, which he recommends for people with cardiac problems. He distills oil extracted from the herb, then roasts some of the plant's green leaves. Whatever gray ash is left over from the roasting Nintzel soaks in vodka to leach out the salts. The finished product is a mixture of the oil, the salts, and the vodka.

"neo-Rosicrucian," came into possession of a manuscript written in a strange coded language. According to Westcott's account, he eventually deciphered the code and found that he had in hand a book of magic rituals. He also said he found hidden between its pages a small scrap of paper with a terse note written on it by a Fräulein Anna Sprengel, with her address in Germany. Westcott said he wrote to her and Sprengel replied, urging him to form an English chapter of an old mystical society—the Golden Dawn.

There seems to be little doubt that Westcott created the fiction of Fräulein Sprengel; perhaps he also wrote the coded manuscript. At any rate, within a few years four branches of the Golden Dawn had been formed and more than 300 people had been initiated. The philosophy of the society was a complicated stew of Freemasonry and occult teachings. Its stated objectives were prosecuting the great work, obtaining control of nature and power over oneself, and "establishing closer and more personal relations with the Lord Jesus."

The Golden Dawn's exacting standards of knowledge and its strict hierarchy distinguished it from the hordes of informal spiritualist organizations that flourished at the time. In its heyday, the society was likened to a Hermetic university. New members had to work their way up through ten levels of enlightenment. After the sixth level, called adeptus minor, they could apply for admission to a more secret stage, known as the Second Order. It was whispered that beyond the Second Order, a shadowy fellowship called the Secret Chiefs went about its business on an otherworldly, astral plane.

One of the Golden Dawn's earliest members was William A. Ayton, a London clergyman. Ayton, who had a formidable knowledge of alchemy and the occult, maintained a laboratory in his cellar and claimed to have actually manufactured the elixir of life. "A French alchemist said it had the right smell and the right color," he revealed to the poet Yeats, "but the first effect of the elixir is that your nails fall out and your hair falls off." Still, Ayton had stored the concoction on a shelf to drink when he became an old man.

Is the Stradivarius's Song an Alchemical Secret?

Almost 300 years after their creation by the Italian master Antonio Stradivari, instruments like the one shown here still represent the very pinnacle of the violinmaker's art. Yet few experts agree which physical properties of a Stradivari violin—usually Latinized to Stradivarius—produce its famous resonant tone. One of the more intriguing proposed solutions to this riddle comes from biochemist Joseph Nagyvary of Texas A & M University, whose explanation draws on Europe's ample alchemical tradition.

Nagyvary's analysis suggests that the exquisite sound of a Stradivarius results in large part from its varnish, a resinous oil that is impregnated with finely powdered quartz, feldspar, and similar minerals. These trace substances, he argues, add just enough rigidity to the violins to produce a voice that is strong but not strident. Creating the critically important mineral dust would have been no simple task, however. The individual fragments are so small that they imply the use of levigation, a highly skilled alchemical process in which the substance to be ground is suspended in a fluid that will catch and hold even the tiniest flakes. Nagyvary thinks Stradivari may well have hired a specialist in the alchemical arts to create the powder for him.

Nagyvary has also tried to apply his findings to contemporary instruments. By combining a special wood treatment and the alchemical varnish, he hopes modern instrument makers may one day duplicate the song—if not the mystique—of a Stradivari violin.

Unfortunately, he continued, "when I got it down the other day it had all dried up."

The Golden Dawn began to unravel only a few years after it was established. By 1900, Samuel Liddell Mathers, who headed up its Paris lodge, had grown highly dictatorial and unpredictable. At one point, he claimed to be the only member to have been inducted into an even higher Third Order by "hidden and unknown Maji." Mathers dispatched the infamous occult figure Aleister Crowley (variously described as a psychopath and the Antichrist) to take over the London lodge. When Crowley arrived wearing a black mask and a Scottish kilt, and armed with a golden dagger, he was summarily rejected and Mathers's lodge was disbanded. By 1905, Yeats had also resigned, the alchemist Ayton had met no further success mixing the elixir of life, and the mystical order itself had all but dried up.

Highly publicized and poorly understood efforts like those of the Golden Dawn did alchemy few favors in the early twentieth century. However, the same period also saw the birth of modern psychology, which—in the view of some circles, at least—would soon lend a new respectability to the Hermetic art. When the spiritual alchemists claimed that the proper end of alchemy was knowing and changing oneself, they had anticipated the expressed goal of the new psychological science. Some psychoanalysts, struggling to find their way along the frontier of the human psyche, employed aspects of alchemical teaching to plumb the human spirit and condition.

Herbert Silberer, an Austrian psychoanalyst, was the first to subject alchemy to a modern psychoanalytical interpretation. He had read Hitchcock and concurred that alchemy's objective was to transform human consciousness. In addition, Silberer believed that the symbolism of alchemy could be analyzed according to the revolutionary methods of his mentor, Dr. Sigmund Freud.

Freud had proposed that in order to live with one another in civilized society, people were forced to curb their more aggressive, animalistic tendencies. These suppressed emotions surfaced in dreams, in which wishes that could not practically be fulfilled in everyday life were symbolically granted. According to Freud's line of reasoning, myths and legends also expressed suppressed wishes, not of individuals but of entire cultures. Assuming that alchemy could easily be counted as a myth, the dutiful Silberer subjected an alchemical parable from eighteenth-century Germany to a thorough Freudian analysis in his 1917 book, *Problems of Mysticism and Its Symbolism* (later republished as *Hidden Symbolism of Alchemy and the Occult Arts).* The parable was about a man who takes an unexpected path in a forest and finds himself involved in a series of adventures, including slaying a lion and rescuing a young woman in distress.

In Silberer's interpretation, this seemingly innocent fairy tale took on frightening dimensions as evidence of humanity's dark and widespread psychosexual desires. Wrote Silberer, "the fugitive impulses and tendencies that seek the darkness and dare not come forth by day . . . have to approach, as it were, in costumes, or disguised as symbols or allegories." The rescue of the parable's damsel in distress represented to Silberer the Oedipus complex (the desire of boys to kill their fathers and marry their mothers).

Although he was committed to a strictly scientific approach, Silberer—like Hitchcock before him—seemed deeply affected by his alchemical-psychoanalytical analysis. In order to understand firsthand how thoughts changed into symbols, he would force himself to write when he was on the verge of sleep, and his thoughts would erupt in weird dreamlike images, which he dutifully recorded in his notes. The more time he spent with alchemical material, the further Silberer strayed from the strict Freudian path. Still later, he was led to believe that alchemical symbolism ultimately addressed issues of higher human experience that could not be psychoanalyzed. "To be sure," he observed near the end of his book, "the final outcome of the work can be summed up in the three words: Union with God." When Silberer presented this hard-earned conclusion to his mentor, Freud dismissed him out of hand. Heartbroken, Silberer eventually committed suicide.

Of all the psychological interpretations of alchemy, the definitive one belongs to the Swiss pioneer of his own special brand of psychoanalysis, Carl Gustav Jung. Jung employed empirical evidence to argue that alchemy was much more than an outmoded forerunner of science. Like Silberer, he began his career under Sigmund Freud and was

Mary Anne South Atwood wrote her scholarly Suggestive Inquiry to show "that the Art of Alchemy was a true Art; and that the Stone of the Philosophers is not a chimera." She later destroyed copies to shield her book away from "an incapable and reckless world."

the eminent man's leading disciple for about five years. Jung was disturbed, however, by Freud's insistence that all human behavior could be reduced to sexual repression and childhood trauma. He was convinced that people were more complex than that, and he said so in his 1912 book, *The Psychology of the Unconscious.* Freud, who brooked no heresy, promptly dissolved their professional and personal relationship.

Jung fared considerably better than the hapless Silberer; his career blossomed as he developed psychological theories beyond anything Freud dared to dream—and in the view of Freud and others, beyond the boundaries of reason. Where Freud saw the unconscious as the repository of an individual's experience, Jung believed that buried deeper down in each person's psyche was the collective unconscious, an inherited repository of universal human experience reaching back to the dawn of the species. In other words, just as everybody has two arms and legs, so everybody has a fundamentally similar, inherited psychic makeup.

Jung had no firm evidence for his convictions, but he eventually came to believe that alchemy provided the proof he needed. In his memoirs he wrote that for a long time he considered alchemy as "something off the beaten path and rather silly." But at some deeper level, he must have been drawn to the ancient art, for he claimed to have had several dreams that prefigured his "discovery" of alchemy. One dream repeated itself numerous times: "Beside my house stood another . . . wing or annex, which was strange to me . . . I discovered there a wonderful library, dating largely from the sixteenth and seventeenth centuries. Among them were a number of books embellished with . . . curious symbols such as I had never seen before . . . only much later did I recognize them as alchemical symbols."

Seeking Proof of Celestial Influence

Lilly Kolisko was an iconoclastic scientific investigator who dedicated years of lab research to proving one of alchemy's most cherished precepts: that earthly metals are influenced by the sun, moon, and planets. Oddly enough, her motivation had nothing to do with alchemical traditions.

A native of Vienna, born in 1889, she was a follower of Austrian spiritualist Rudolf Steiner and conducted her study at his bidding. Steiner is best remembered for his theories on education, but he was also a believer in unseen spiritual forces, which—he was convinced—interacted with everything in nature. One of his pet theories dealt with the influence of the solar system in the formation of metals. In his view, the minerals in the earth's crust once existed in a fluid state. Before they became solidified, he felt, they were

The image below was produced in one of Lilly Kolisko's capillary-dynamolysis experiments, performed on Easter Sunday of 1929. She used filter paper to soak up a solution of gold chloride and studied the resulting bands of color.

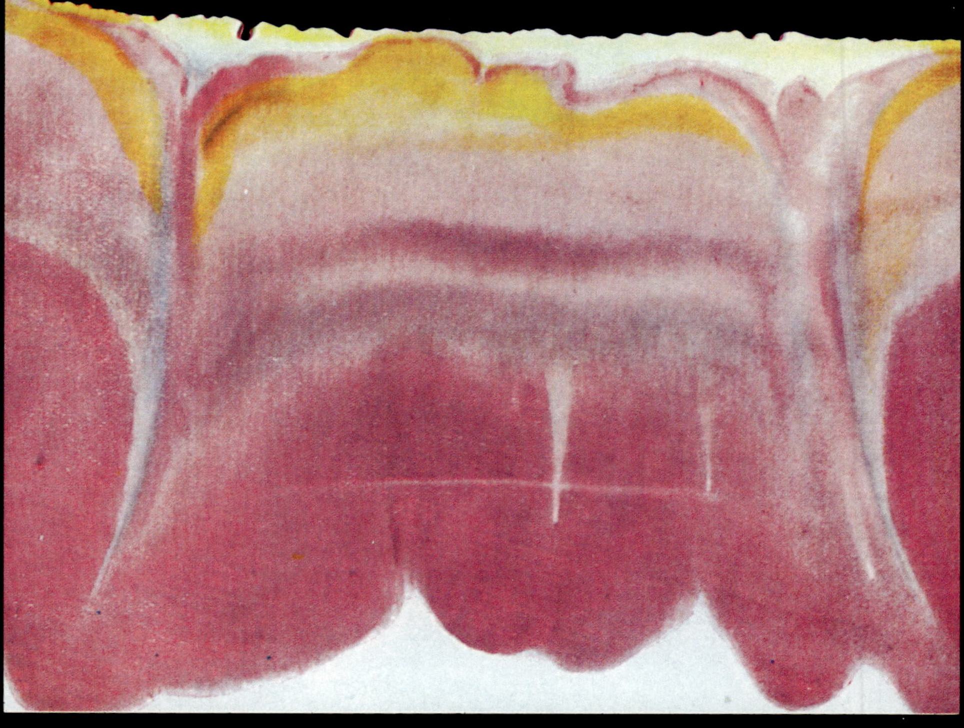

In another dream, Jung found himself on the Italian front in the middle of World War I, trying to outrace the battle in a horse-drawn wagon driven by a peasant. The wagon eventually entered a beautiful, peaceful landscape that Jung recognized as the region of Verona. In order to get to the city, they had to pass through the courtyard of a duke's palace. "Just as we reached the middle of the courtyard . . . both gates flew shut. The peasant leaped down from his seat and exclaimed, 'Now we are caught in the seventeenth century.' " Jung believed that the dream was a reference to alchemy, which reached its height in the seventeenth century.

In 1928, Jung received a book about ancient Chinese alchemy from Sinologist Richard Wilhelm. Within a few years, Jung had assembled a real library of books on alchemy much like the one in his earlier dream. "One night, while I was studying them, I suddenly recalled the dream that I was caught in the seventeenth century. At last I grasped its meaning. 'So that's it! Now I am condemned to study alchemy from the very beginning!' " Jung discovered that alchemy was remarkably similar to his own theories of analytic psychology. The Hermetic tradition provided Jung with what he considered his missing link, tying his new psychological theories to an intellectual chord that reached back to Greek philosophy.

Students of spiritual alchemy like Hitchcock and Silberer contended that true alchemists had never attempted physical transmutations—indeed, that they had invented stories of physical alchemy to mask their real goals of inner, spiritual transformation. Jung, on the other hand, contended that alchemists *had* performed physical experiments and that they had created—or imagined that they had created—real gold out of baser metals. He argued that the alchemists of

imbued with the spirits of neighboring stars and planets, and they continue to respond to earth's heavenly neighbors.

To Kolisko fell the challenging task of proving this cosmological interconnectedness, using scientific methods. To do so, she devised an ingenious though—most would say—inconclusive laboratory procedure called capillary dynamolysis.

Several times a day, for weeks and months on end, she dissolved small amounts of metallic compounds—gold chloride, iron sulfate, silver nitrate—in measured amounts of water. In each solution, she stood on end a rolled-up strip of chemists' filter paper to absorb the liquid. When the carefully dated and timed filters were unrolled, they exhibited distinctive patterns of color *(below)* brought about when the various components of a solution were leached up to different levels in the paper. As planetary conditions shifted during the year, Kolisko studied these patterns and charted the changes she detected. After two years, she had learned to recognize the distinctive patterns of the metals and claimed she could deduce the time of year at which particular samplings were made.

Kolisko's work was highly esteemed by Rudolf Steiner, who considered it definitive proof of the powers exerted by celestial bodies. But the scientific community never took much notice of her study.

The same experiment carried out on Christmas of 1929 produced a markedly different color pattern. Kolisko attributed the changes to differences in the influence of the sun—the heavenly body associated with gold—on the two dates in question.

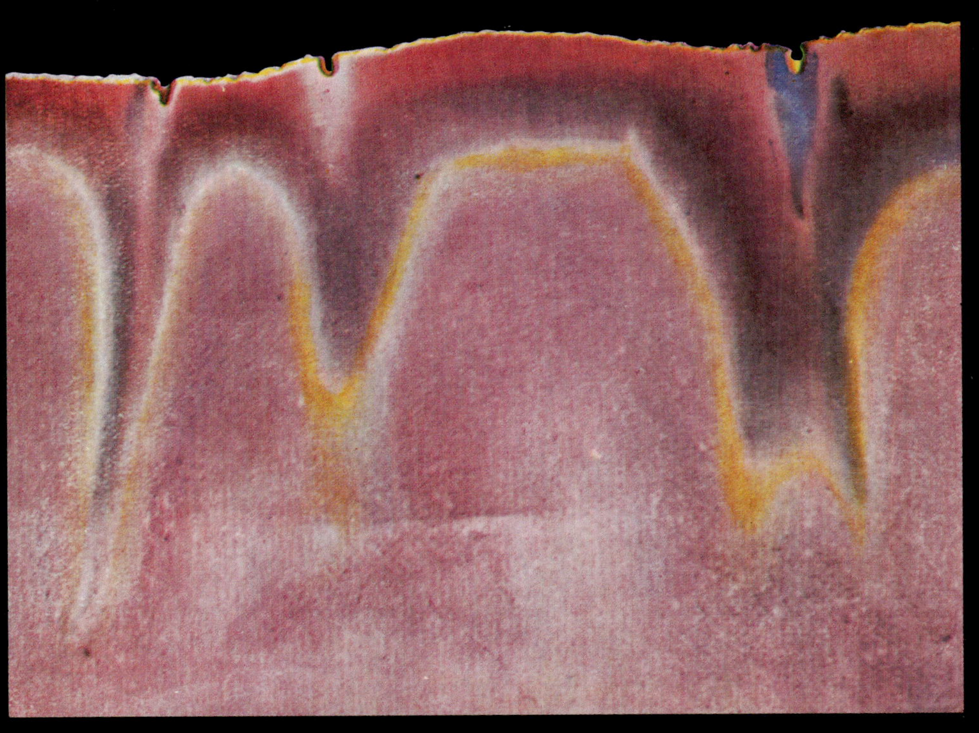

old worked with little knowledge of physical chemistry and no inkling of their deeper psychological drives. As they struggled to perfect the great work, their unconscious minds would project their inner fantasies of perfection onto their laboratory results. The miraculous transformations they "saw" with their eyes reflected the deeper transformations occurring in their personalities.

Jung began to realize that the fantastic dream images he collected from his modern patients in therapy often contained symbols identical to those of alchemy, even if the patients had no conscious knowledge of the Hermetic art. These dream pictures included the cosmic tree growing from the roots of its upside-down mirror image (symbolizing the alchemical verity of "as above, so below," said Jung), various representations of the union of opposites, and symbols for the ancient traditional elements of earth, air, water, and fire. When Jung published these findings in his 1946 book, *Psychology and Alchemy,* he boldly declared that his own science of depth psychology was nothing more than the age-old practice of alchemy enwrapped in twentieth century garb.

Jung also attempted to tie the Hermetic art to modern physics. In one of his later books, which was titled *Mysterium Coniunctionis,* he proposed that the collective unconscious encompassed not only human psychology but the entire universe just the same. Recalling the microcosm/

Making an Elixir Known as Vegetable Gold

In 1960, after years of Hermetic labor, Frenchman Armand Barbault produced his first batch of "Vegetable gold." His method was modeled on the great work as revealed in the *Mutus Liber (pages 70-77)* and other esoteric sources. He claimed to have extracted "the soul of gold," a medicine that would enable the body "to combat decay."

Barbault was a well-known astrologer in France when his second wife, Jacqueline, persuaded him to move to the country and devote himself to alchemy. In 1948, at a time and a place determined astrologically, the pair collected some four pounds of so-called living earth, or philosophers' peat, which they felt was "charged with the forces of life." For the next twelve years, in alchemical processes pictured at right and on the following pages, the couple tended and manipulated this material until it gave up its golden liquid. Their labors came to include their son, Alexandre *(far right).*

Barbault was troubled by a weakness of the heart that began when he was a young man and suffered an electric shock of 1,500 volts. Despite his cardiac problems, he lived to be sixty-eight, a fact that Alexandre, who became a physician, attributed to his father's regular use of the elixir.

Collecting dew so as to capture its "etheric forces," Barbault drags a canvas over grass before sunrise on a cloudless spring morning. *Fifty yards'* dragging would yield about a quart of dew.

macrocosm schema of traditional alchemy, Jung suggested that the universe outside was also the world inside the mind; that is, the two were indistinguishable.

Thus alchemy, which had evolved slowly over the ages, experienced rapid upheavals in the fast-paced twentieth century. Modern alchemists continued to work in laboratories very similar to those of their forebears, but they made a craft once available to only a few select initiates accessible to anyone willing to study. They also extended the applications of their labors, attempting to bring alchemy to bear on the problems of the modern world. In fact, many who today call themselves alchemists seem unconcerned with traditional physical goals, and their spiritual training is not so much an introspective study as a redefining of values.

One of America's most renowned twentieth-century alchemists, Albert Riedel, was born in Dresden, Germany, in 1911. Riedel came to the United States when he was seventeen and lived in California for many years before founding the Paracelsus Research Society in Salt Lake City under a new name he selected for himself, Frater Albertus.

Albertus was reportedly a harsh taskmaster. As one follower said, "His method was true to the code of alchemy: to not give anything away on a platter, but to make you work for it. To *sweat* for it." He taught his students to employ their alchemy primarily on plants, applying the theory

Barbault and his son wring out the dew from a wet canvas. The dew collected on the cloth must not touch the ground, Barbault warned, "or all etheric forces will immediately return to earth."

Father and son collect strong young plants just before sunrise. The plants are chosen the previous day, Barbault said, and "ordered to draw greater force from the ground" for the alchemist's use.

of Basil Valentine and other antecedents that all matter was composed of sulfur (representing the soul), mercury (the spirit), and salt (the body, or "vehicle of transformation").

In Frater Albertus's laboratories, disciples practiced a "three-fold process of separation" on herbs and succulents, extracting the "soul" and "spirit" and burning the leftovers to purify the "body." These three "essentials" were reconstituted into a substance called plant stone, which, according to a complex correspondence between the original plant and specific parts of the body, served as a powerful medicine. Tincture of rosemary, for example, was said to be good for the heart.

The Paracelsus Society enjoyed its heyday in the 1960s and 1970s, when it offered seminars to hundreds of enthusiasts and published a quarterly called *Parachemy.* Art Kunkin, who had founded the *Los Angeles Free Press* in the 1960s, visited Albertus in 1980. Afterward he attempted some alchemical experiments on his own and claimed that by placing manganese in a petri dish with some bacteria, he successfully transmuted it into iron. Moreover, he said that research into respected academic journals revealed to him that a U.S. Army unit in Virginia had successfully performed the same experiment. (The army was supposedly interested in capturing the energy produced by transmutation to power longer-lasting batteries.)

Kunkin was so impressed that he decided to pack up

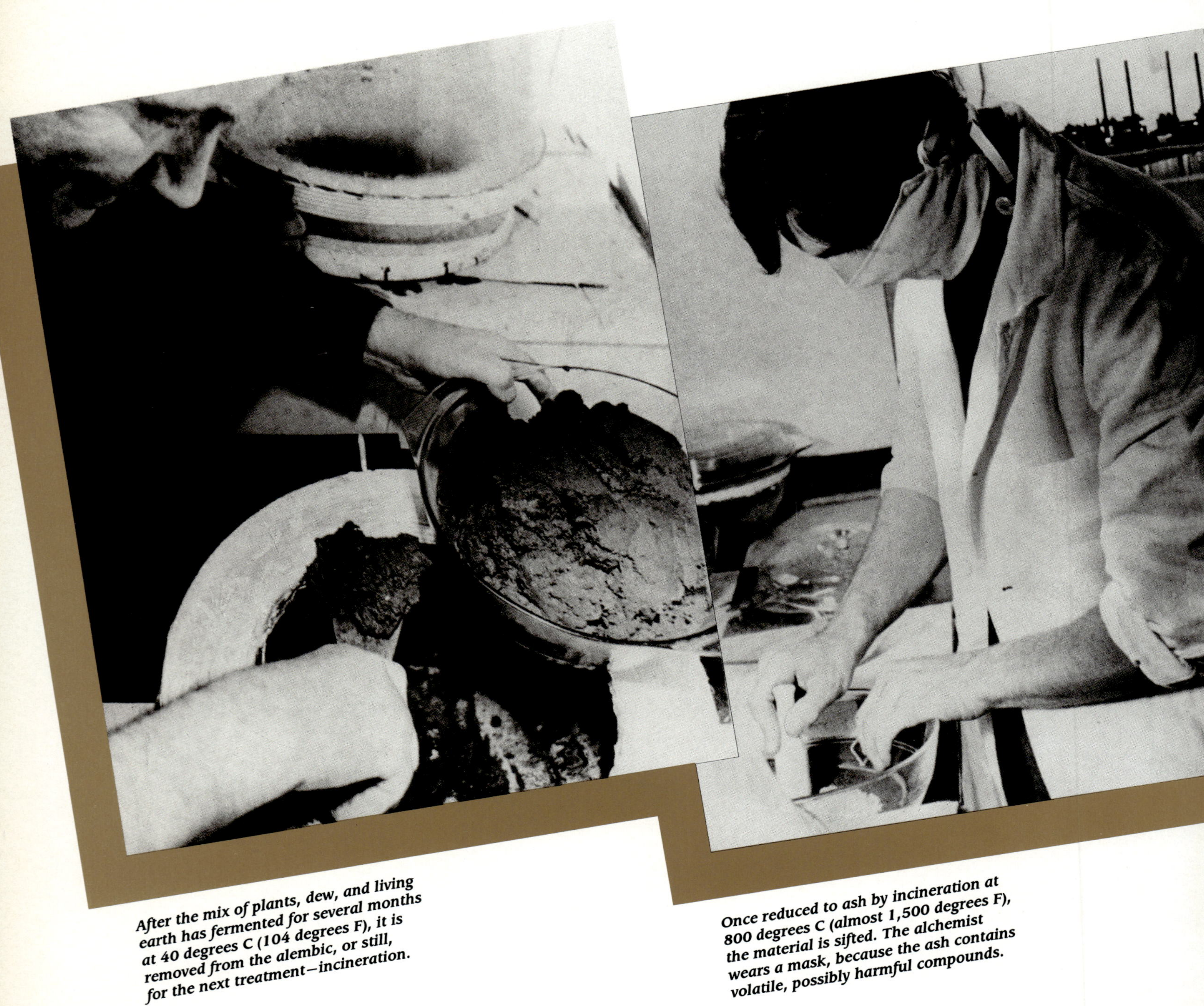

After the mix of plants, dew, and living earth has fermented for several months at 40 degrees C (104 degrees F), it is removed from the alembic, or still, for the next treatment—incineration.

Once reduced to ash by incineration at 800 degrees C (almost 1,500 degrees F), the material is sifted. The alchemist wears a mask, because the ash contains volatile, possibly harmful compounds.

and move to Salt Lake City permanently, when he received a phone call from some students at the society warning that Frater Albertus was not a genuine adept. Far from being a spiritual master, said these disillusioned devotees, Albertus was a fraud and "the Devil." But Kunkin was determined to learn alchemy; he replied that if Albertus was the devil, then he would "go to study with the Devil."

Although he found no Satan, Kunkin learned the hard way that Frater Albertus was stingy with his knowledge. "Frater's nature was to teach up to a certain point," recalled Kunkin, "then he would freeze up and nothing more would be forthcoming." Albertus's secrecy and egotism eventually drove Kunkin back to California. The Paracelsus Society appears to have perished with the death of Frater Albertus in 1984, although some of his followers went on to other alchemical pursuits.

Some people who have called themselves alchemists in the late twentieth century have forsaken sensational transmutations altogether, basing their work instead on modern science aimed toward goals compatible with traditional alchemical ideals. In 1970, the New Alchemy Institute was established on Cape Cod, Massachusetts. Founded by several former biology professors and their friends, the New Alchemy Institute "transmuted" common resources into useful products that would not damage the environment. Their goal was to transform people's attitudes in order that

Barbault slides a test tube full of ash, dew, and powdered gold into a circular oven. This mixture is boiled for four hours and then cooled for four hours, in a cycle that is repeated seven times.

Father and son examine "the liquor of Gold," filtered from the mixture that was cooked in the test tubes. When "the Elixir is perfect," said Barbault, "a symbolic Star is seen floating on the surface."

the human race might live in a "gentle, environmentally sound manner."

The New Alchemists were a far from secret group. They made every effort to reach out to the larger community—even collaborating with the Massachusetts Department of Food and Agriculture and its Bureau of Solid Waste Management. In 1976, the institute's members built the Cape Cod Ark, in effect a large greenhouse—they called it a bioshelter—that functioned as a self-contained environment, heated in the winter by solar algae ponds and heat-absorbent rock piles. Temperate-zone crops were planted near the ark's floor, and more tropical varieties were positioned up near its skylights. The algae ponds served both as fish farms and as vegetable gardens. Over the years the institute attracted visitors from across the United States, who came to learn about everything from recycling to solar-housing designs.

The New Alchemists hoped by all these efforts to "transform something ordinary into something valuable" and to restore a balance between human beings and their world—objectives that sound much like the aspirations of alchemists throughout history.

The New Alchemists took a risk in evoking the image of the old Hermetic practitioners in the name they selected for their realistic and scientific enterprise. For all its rich and impressive history, alchemy still carries a stigma. The most extreme examples of alchemical credulity are those that receive the most attention, so it is not surprising that alchemists continue to struggle for respect. And there remain enormous, perhaps unbridgeable, gaps between the perspective of mainstream scientists and that of alchemists.

At the same time, however, scientists who once scoffed at the prospect of turning dross into gold now regularly perform such feats. With the advent of enormous and highly advanced particle colliders, physicists and engineers have rendered physical transmutations an everyday occurrence. Scientists are quick to point out that the goals of alchemy remain impractical, because even with current methods it would cost trillions of dollars to transmute some other substance into a pound of gold. Nevertheless, through the knowledge gained by high-tech transmutations, science is hot on the trail of another age-old alchemical goal: discovering the basic building blocks of the universe.

In October 1989, particle-collision experiments carried out simultaneously in the United States and Europe revealed what scientists believed to be the entire range of irreducible particles in existence. They reported that the subatomic particles—protons, neutrons, and electrons—were further divided into three "families" of *sub*-subatomic particles. One category of these infinitesimal specks of matter, the quarks, had been posited since the mid-1960s. They were christened with names that sound as if they were lifted from an alchemist's notebook—names such as charmed, strange, truth, beauty.

Scientists defend such labels as pure whimsy, but it is fair to say that the further scientific knowledge advances, the less certain scientists become about what is "real." Contemporary scientific theories about the nature of the universe sound every bit as strange as the most exalted notions of alchemy. Astronomers now brood about antimatter and time warps. A physicist at Johns Hopkins University who worked with a California particle collider said he was searching for "a field that pervades all existence and gives particles their mass."

If anything, contemporary science has reinforced the old alchemical notion of the microcosm of humankind projecting itself out onto the macrocosm of universe. Scientists admit that, at both the subatomic and the galactic levels, it is increasingly difficult to distinguish what they think they observe from what they expect, or hope, to find. No less an authority than the Nobel physicist Eugene Wigner asserted that what we call physical objects have much in common with spiritual values.

From such a statement it requires only a small step to contemplate the notion that human knowledge has not progressed along a straight line but rather has come full circle to the understanding of the alchemists of old.

A supernova, the ultimate crucible, glows with energy released by transmutation of elements deep within. In such a stellar explosion—this one is Supernova 1987A, the first observed in 1987—the alchemist's dream comes true: Heat and pressure combine to forge gold and all the other elements of creation. But at the same time, the exploding star turns gold into lead.

ACKNOWLEDGMENTS

The editors would like to thank the following for their assistance in the preparation of this volume: Dr. Paul Arnold, Director, Staatliche Kunstsammlungen, Dresden; Dr. Alexandre Barbault, Colmar, France; Paola Forneris, Biblioteca Civica, San Remo, Italy; Marie Odile Germain, Conservateur, Département des Manuscrits, Bibliothèque Nationale, Paris; Dr. Nina Gockerell, Bayerisches Nationalmuseum, Munich; Reiner Grosz, Director, Staatsarchiv, Dresden; Elizabeth Heidt, Süddeutscher Verlag Bilderdienst, Munich; Heidi Klein, Bildarchiv Preussischer Kulturbesitz, West Berlin; Gabrielle Kohler, Archiv für Kunst und Geschichte, West Berlin; Michael Kowalski, Deutsches Apotheken-Museum, Heidelberg; Dany Lecco, Conservateur, Département des Manuscrits, Bibliothèque Nationale, Paris; Adam McLean, Oxford; Gianbattista Marassi, Cremona, Italy; Hans W. Nintzel, Richardson, Texas; Günter Probeck, Deutsches Museum, Munich; Dr. W. Ryan, London; Barbara A. Shattuck, *National Geographic,* Washington, D.C.

BIBLIOGRAPHY

Allen, Judy, and Jeanne Griffiths, *The Book of the Dragon.* London: Orbis, 1979.

Angrist, Stanley W., "Perpetual Motion Machines." *Scientific American,* January 1968.

Ashmole, Elias, *Theatrum Chemicum Britannicum.* London: Nash Brooks, 1652.

Atwood, Mary Anne South, *A Suggestive Inquiry into Hermetic Philosophy and Alchemy.* New York: Arno Press, 1976 (reprint of 1920 edition).

Aylesworth, Thomas G., *The Alchemists: Magic into Science.* Reading, Mass.: Addison-Wesley, 1973.

Barbault, Armand, *Gold of a Thousand Mornings.* Transl. by Robin Campbell. London: Neville Spearman, 1975.

Bolton, Henry Carrington, *The Follies of Science at the Court of Rudolph II.* Milwaukee: Pharmaceutical Review, 1904.

Booth, William, "Battling Scientists Agree on the Nature of Matter." *The Washington Post,* October 14, 1989.

Buchanan, Keith, Charles P. FitzGerald, and Colin A. Ronan, *China.* New York: Crown, 1981.

Burland, C. A., *The Arts of the Alchemists.* London: Weidenfeld and Nicolson, 1967.

Caron, M., and S. Hutin, *The Alchemists.* Transl. by Helen R. Lane. New York: Grove Press, 1961.

Cattell, J. McKeen, ed., "The Transmutation of Mercury into Gold." *Scientific Monthly,* November 1925.

Cohen, I. Bernard:
Album of Science: From Leonardo to Lavoisier, 1450-1800. New York: Charles Scribner's Sons, 1980.
Ethan Allen Hitchcock: Soldier, Humanitarian, Scholar. Worcester, Mass.: The Society, 1952.

Debus, Allen G., *The English Paracelsians.* New York: Franklin Watts, 1965.

de Yonge, Alex, and Norman Gelb, transls., *Gold* (exhibition catalog). New York: Alpine Fine Arts Collection, 1981.

Doberer, K. K., *The Goldmakers: 10,000 Years of Alchemy.* Westport, Conn.: Greenwood Press, 1972.

Dubs, Homer H., "The Origin of Alchemy." *Ambix,* February 1961.

Dunleavy, Gareth W., "The Chaucer Ascription in Trinity College, Dublin." *Ambix,* February 1965.

Editors of Time-Life Books, *Stars* (Voyage through the Universe series). Alexandria, Va.: Time-Life Books, 1989.

Eliade, Mircea:
The Forge and the Crucible. Transl. by Stephen Corrin. London: Rider, 1962.
"The Myth of Alchemy." *Parabola,* Vol. 3, no. 3.

Federman, Reinhard, *The Royal Art of Alchemy.* Transl. by Richard H. Weber. Philadelphia: Chilton, 1969.

Foote, Paul D., "The Alchemist." *Scientific Monthly,* September 1924.

Franz, Marie-Louise von, "The Idea of the Macro- and Microcosms in the Light of Jungian Psychology." *Ambix,* February 1965.

French, Peter, *John Dee: The World of an Elizabethan Magus.* New York: Ark Paperbacks, 1978.

Fulcannelli, *Le Mystère des Cathédrales.* Transl. by Mary Sworder. Albuquerque, N.M.: Brotherhood of Life, 1986.

Godwin, Joscelyn, *Robert Fludd: Hermetic Philosopher and Surveyor of Two Worlds.* London: Thames and Hudson, 1979.

Hamblin, Dora Jane, "Wood and Dedication in Old Cremona." *Smithsonian,* October 1983.

Higby, Gregory J., "Gold in Medicine: A Review of Its Use in the West before 1900." *Gold Bulletin,* Vol. 15, 1982.

Hill, W. Henry, Arthur F. Hill, and Alfred E. Hill, *Antonio Stradivari: His Life and Work (1644-1737).* New York: Dover, 1902.

Hitchcock, Ethan Allen, *Alchemy and the Alchemists.* Los Angeles: Philosophical Research Society, 1976 (reprint of 1857 edition).

Hoeller, Stephan A., "C. G. Jung and the Alchemical Renewal." *Gnosis,* summer 1988.

Holmyard, Eric John:
Alchemy. Baltimore: Penguin, 1968.
Makers of Chemistry. London: Oxford University Press, 1962 (reprint of 1931 edition).

Hopkins, Arthur John, *Alchemy: Child of Greek Philosophy.* New York: AMS Press, 1967.

Howe, Ellic, *The Magicians of the Golden Dawn.* London: Routledge & Kegan Paul, 1972.

Howe, Ellic, ed., *The Alchemist of the Golden Dawn.* Wellingborough, Northamptonshire, England: Aquarian Press, 1988.

Ihde, Aaron J., *The Development of Modern Chemistry.* New York: Harper & Row, 1964.

Inglis, Brian, *A History of Medicine.* Cleveland: World, 1965.

Jaffe, Bernard, "The Human Crucible." *The Forum,* May 1930.

Johnson, Kenneth Rayner, *The Fulcanelli Phenomenon.* Jersey, Channel Islands: Neville Spearman, 1980.

Johnson, Obed Simon, *A Study of Chinese Alchemy.* Shanghai, China: Commercial Press, 1928.

Jung, C. G., *Memories, Dreams, and Reflections.* New York: Vintage Books, 1961.

Kean, W. F., et al., "The History of Gold Therapy in Rheumatoid Disease." *Seminars in Arthritis and Rheumatism,* February 1985.

Kirshner, Robert P., "Supernova: Death of a Star." *National Geographic,* May 1988.

Klossowski de Rola, Stanislas, *Alchemy: The Secret Art.* London: Thames and Hudson, 1985.

Koenig, Robert A., "The Alchemy Institute." *New Realities,* September-October 1988.

Kolisko, L.:
Spirit in Matter: A Scientist's Answer to the Bishop's Queries. Stroud, England: Kolisko Archive, 1948.
Workings of the Stars in Earthly Substances. London: Orient-Occident, 1928.

Kolisko, L., Adalbert Stifter, and Rudolf Steiner, *The Sun Eclipse.* Transl. by G. A. M. Knapp and Susan Stern. Bournemouth, England: Kolisko Archive, 1978.

Lai, T. C., *The Eight Immortals.* Kowloon, Hong Kong: Swindon, 1972.

Lennep, Jacques van, *Alchimie.* Brussels, Belgium: Crédit Communal de Belgique, 1985.

Lindsay, Jack, *The Origins of Alchemy in Graeco-Roman Egypt.* New York: Barnes & Noble, 1970.

Loewe, Michael, *Ways to Paradise: The Chinese Quest for Immortality.* London: George Allen & Unwin, 1979.

Lurker, Manfred, *The Gods and Symbols of Ancient Egypt: An Illustrated Dictionary.* London: Thames and Hudson, 1974.

McLean, Adam, *A Commentary on the Mutus Liber.* Edinburgh, Scotland: Magnum Opus Hermetic Sourceworks, 1982.

Marx, Jenifer, *The Magic of Gold.* Garden City, N.Y.: Doubleday, 1978.

Multhauf, Robert P., *The Origins of Chemistry.* New York: Franklin Watts, 1967.

Nagyvary, Joseph, "The Chemistry of a Stradivarius." *Chemical and Engineering News,* May 23, 1988.

Nagyvary, Joseph, and J. M. Ehrman, "The Composite Nature of the Antique Italian Varnish." *Naturwissenschaften,* October 1988.

Nicholl, Charles, *The Chemical Theatre.* London: Routledge & Kegan Paul, 1980.

Nintzel, Hans, "Alchemy Is Alive and Well." *Gnosis,* summer 1988.

Ord-Hume, Arthur W. J. G., *Perpetual Motion: The History of an Obsession.* London: George Allen & Unwin, 1977.

Pagel, Walter, *Paracelsus: An Introduction to Philosophical Medicine in the Era of the Renaissance.* New York: Karger, 1982.

Paneth, Fritz:
"Ancient and Modern Alchemy." *Science,* October 29, 1926.
"The Transmutation of Hydrogen into Helium." *Nature,* May 14, 1927.

Paracelsus, *Selected Writings.* Ed. by Jolande Jacobi. Transl. by Norbert Guterman. Princeton, N.J.: Princeton University Press, 1979.

Partington, J. R., *A Short History of Chemistry.* New York: Harper & Brothers, 1960.

Pauwels, Louis, and Jacques Bergier, *The Morning of the Magicians.* Transl. by Rollo Myers. New York: Dorset Press, 1988.

Pearsall, Ronald, *The Alchemists.* London: Weidenfeld and Nicolson, 1976.

Po-tuan, Chang, *Understanding Reality.* Transl. by Thomas Cleary. Honolulu: University of Hawaii Press, 1987.

Powell, Neil, *Alchemy, the Ancient Science.* Garden City, N.Y.: Doubleday, 1976.

Ramsey, William, "Modern Transmutation of the Elements." *National Geographic,* April 1966.

Rawson, Philip, and Laszlo Legeza, *Tao: The Chinese Philosophy of Time and Change.* London: Thames and Hudson, 1973.

Read, John:
Prelude to Chemistry: An Outline of Alchemy. Cambridge, Mass.: M.I.T. Press, 1966 (reprint of 1936 edition).
Through Alchemy to Chemistry: A Procession of Ideas & Personalities. London: G. Bell and Sons, 1961.
Redgrove, H. Stanley, *Alchemy: Ancient and Modern*. New Hyde Park, N.Y.: University Books, 1969.
"The Reported Transmutation of Mercury into Gold." *Nature*, August 9, 1924.
"The Retreat of the Modern Alchemists." *Scientific American*, January 1928.
Russell, A. S. "The Transmutation of the Elements." *Discovery*, August 1923.
Rutherford, Ernest, "Artificial Disintegration of the Elements." *Journal of the Chemical Society*, Vol. 121, 1922.
Sadoul, Jacques, *Alchemists and Gold*. Transl. by Olga Sieveking. London: Neville Spearman, 1972.
Schafer, Edward H., and the Editors of Time-Life Books, *Ancient China* (Great Ages of Man series). New York: Time-Life Books, 1967.
Schramm, Petra, *Die Alchemisten*. Wiesbaden, West Germany: Rarissima Taunusstein, 1984.
Shepard, Leslie, *Alchemy: Ancient and Modern*. New Hyde Park, N.Y.: University Books, 1969.
Shepard, Leslie, ed., *Encyclopedia of Occultism & Parapsychology*. Vol. 3. Detroit: Gale Research, 1984.
Sherlock, T. P., "The Chemical Work of Paracelsus." *Ambix*, May 1948.
Sherr, R., et al., "Transmutation of Mercury by Fast Neutrons." *The Physical Review*, October 1, 1941.
Shumaker, Wayne, *The Occult Sciences in the Renaissance*. Los Angeles: University of California Press, 1972.
Silberer, Herbert, *Hidden Symbolism of Alchemy and the Occult Arts*. Transl. by Smith Ely Jelliffe. New York: Dover, 1971 (reprint of 1917 edition).
Sivin, Nathan:
Chinese Alchemy: Preliminary Studies. Cambridge, Mass.: Harvard University Press, 1968.
Traditional Medicine in Contemporary China. Ann Arbor, Mich.: University of Michigan, 1987.
Sivin, Nathan, ed., *Science and Technology in East Asia*. New York: Science History Publications, 1977.
Smits, A., and A. Karssen, "Cracking the Lead Atom." *Scientific American*, October 1925.
Soddy, Frederick, "The Reported Transmutation of Mercury into Gold." *Nature*, August 16, 1924.
Spielberg, Nathan, and Bryon D. Anderson, *Seven Ideas That Shook the Universe*. New York: John Wiley & Sons, 1987.
Stillman, John Maxson, *The Story of Alchemy and Early Chemistry*. New York: Dover, 1960.
Sworder, Mary, transl., *Fulcanelli: Master Alchemist*. London: Neville Spearman, no date.
Taylor, Frank Sherwood, *The Alchemists: Founders of Modern Chemistry*. New York: Arno Press, 1974 (reprint of 1949 edition).
"Tests Fail to Confirm Transmutation to Gold." *Scientific American*, November 1925.
Thompson, C. J. S., *The Lure and Romance of Alchemy*. London: George G. Harrap, 1932.
Trowbridge, W. R. H., *Cagliostro*. New Hyde Park, N.Y.: University Books, 1961.
Van Melsen, Andrew G., *From Atomos to Atom: The History of the Concept Atom*. New York: Harper & Brothers, 1960.
Waite, Arthur Edward, *Alchemists through the Ages*. Blauvelt, N.Y.: Rudolf Steiner, 1970.
Waite, Arthur Edward, transl. and ed., *The Alchemical Writings of Edward Kelly*. New York: S. Weiser, 1970 (reprint of 1893 edition).
Ware, James R., transl. and ed., *Alchemy, Medicine and Religion in the China of A.D. 320*. New York: Dover, 1981.
Webster, Charles, *From Paracelsus to Newton: Magic and the Making of Modern Science*. Cambridge: Cambridge University Press, 1982.
Witten II, Laurence C., and Richard Pachella, comp., *Alchemy and the Occult*. Vol. 3. New Haven, Conn.: Yale University Library, 1977.
Yates, Frances Amelia:
The Occult Philosophy in the Elizabethan Age. Boston: Routledge & Kegan Paul, 1979.
The Rosicrucian Enlightenment. Boulder, Colo.: Shambhala, 1978.
Zolla, Elemire, "The Retrieval of Alchemy." *Parabola*, Vol. 3, no. 3.

PICTURE CREDITS

The sources for the pictures in this book are listed below. Credits from left to right are separated by semicolons; credits from top to bottom are separated by dashes.

Cover: Art by Bryan Leister. 6, 7: Münchner Stadtmuseum, Munich. 8: Seth Joel, courtesy The Charles Edwin Wilbour Fund, Brooklyn Museum. 9: C. M. Dixon/Photoresources, Canterbury, England. 10: Gilbert Mangin, Nancy, France. 11: The Metropolitan Museum of Art, Rogers Fund, 1943 (#43.24.3). 12: V. Sarianidi, L. Bogdanov, V. Terebenin, Moscow. 13: Columbia Gold Museum. 15: Henry Groskinsky, courtesy Beinecke Library, Yale University. 16: The Bettmann Archive, New York. 18: Michael Holford, Loughton, Essex, England. 19: Rijksmuseum van Oudheden, Leiden, Netherlands. 22: J. Guillot-Connaissance des Arts/ Edimedia, Paris. 23: Anderson/Alinari, Florence. 24, 25: Artwork by Time-Life Books; Bibliothèque Nationale, Paris. 26, 27: The Fine Art Photographic Library, London. 28: Mirco Toso, courtesy Biblioteca Nazionale Marciana, Venice. 29: Jean-Loup Charmet, Paris. 30-33: The Mary Evans Picture Library, London. 35: Detail from pp. 36-37. 36, 37: Erwin Böhm, courtesy Deutsches Apotheken-Museum im Heidelberger Schloss; painting by Adriaen van Ostade, courtesy The National Gallery, London. 38, 39: Staatliche Kunsthalle Karlsruhe; Erwin Böhm, courtesy Deutsches Apotheken-Museum im Heidelberger Schloss; Deutsches Museum, Munich. 40, 41: Reproduced courtesy the Board of Directors of the Budapest Museum of Fine Arts; Erwin Böhm, courtesy Deutsches Apotheken-Museum im Heidelberger Schloss. 43: Henry Groskinsky, courtesy Beinecke Library, Yale University. 44: Jean-Loup Charmet, Paris. 48-54: Henry Groskinsky, courtesy Beinecke Library, Yale University. 56: Images Colour Library, Leeds, England. 57: Fisher Collection, Fisher Scientific, Pittsburgh. 58: Granger Collection, New York. 59: Images Colour Library, Leeds, England. 60, 61: Fisher Collection, Fisher Scientific, Pittsburgh; Sammlung fü Plastik und Kunstgewerbe, Kunsthistorisches Museum, Vienna. 62: Prokop Paul, Jiri Kopriva, Prague. 65: Claus Hansmann, Munich. 66: From *A History of Medicine* by Brian Inglis, World Publishing Company, Cleveland, 1965—Ulrich Pinder/The Folger Shakespeare Library, Washington, D.C.; from *Album of Science from Leonardo to Lavoisier, 1450-1800* by I. Bernard Cohen, Charles Scribner's Sons, New York, 1980. 67: Robert Fludd, *Intergrum Morborum Mysterium: Sive Medicinae Catholicae,* courtesy Library of Congress. 68: Jean-Loup Charmet, Paris—Städtsiches Reiss-Museum, Mannheim Foto, Erwin Böhm, Mainz, West Germany. 69: The Granger Collection; Luisa Ricciarini, Milan, courtesy Museum Nacional de Arte Antiga, Lisbon, detail from *The Temptation of St. Anthony* by Hieronymus Bosch. 70-77: Details at top of each page, Adam McLean/Magnum Opus Hermetic Sourceworks, Edinburgh—*Alchemy* by Johannes Fabricus, Aquarian Press, Northamptonshire, England, 1976. 79: Kantonsbibliothek (Vadiana), St. Gallen, Switzerland. 80: From *The Golden Game* by Stanislas Klossowski de Rola, George Braziller, New York, 1988. 81: Süddeutscher Verlag Bilderdienst, Munich. 84: The Warburg Institute, London. 85: Bibliotheca Philosophica Hermetica, Amsterdam. 86, 87: Library of Congress. 88: Bayerisches Nationalmuseum, Munich—Staatliche Kunstsammlungen, Dresden. 89: Erich Lessing, Culture and Fine Art Archive, Vienna. 90: Culver Pictures. 91: From *Robert Fludd: Hermetic Philosopher and Surveyor of Two Worlds* by Joscelyn Godwin, Thames and Hudson, London, 1979. 93: Images Colour Library, Leeds, England. 94, 95: From *Perpetual Motion: The History of an Obsession* by Arthur W. J. G. Ord-Hume, George Allen & Unwin, London, 1977. 97: National Portrait Gallery, London; courtesy the Trustees of the British Library, London. 98: The Hulton-Deutsch Collection, London. 99: Erich Lessing, courtesy Kunsthistorisches Museum, Vienna, Muenzkabinett. 100: *Cagliostro: The Splendor and Misery of a Master of Magic* by W. R. H. Trowbridge, University Books, New Hyde Park, N.Y., 1961. 103: Nathan Sivin, ed. *Science and Technology in East Asia,* Science History Publications, New York, 1977. 104: *Tao* by Philip Rawson & Laszlo Legeza, Thames and Hudson, London, 1973—*The Taoist Canon*. 105: Courtesy the Trustees of the British Museum, London. 106: *The Taoist Canon*. 107: Larry Sherer, courtesy Patti Cass. 108, 109: Courtesy the Trustees of the British Museum, London; Victoria and Albert Museum, London; The Oriental Museum, University of Durham, England. 110: Ian Thomas, courtesy the Trustees of the Victoria and Albert Museum, London—Larry Sherer, courtesy Nathan Sivin. 111: MacQuitty International Collection, London. 112: Freer Gallery of Art, Washington, D.C. 113: From *The Eight Immortals* by T. C. Lai, Hong Kong, 1972. 115: Henry Groskinsky, courtesy Beinecke Library, Yale University. 116: Fred Sons. 118: Reproduced from the collections of the Library of Congress, *Scientific American,* November 1925. 120: Ullstein Bilderdienst, West Berlin. 121: Ullstein Bilderdienst, West Berlin—Süddeutscher Verlag Bilderdienst, Munich. 122: Roger-Viollet, Paris. 123: Jean-Loup Charmet, Paris, courtesy Institut National de la Propriété Industrielle. 124, 125: Hubert Josse, Paris, except center Bulloz, Paris. 127: Courtesy Hans Nintzel. 128: Scala, Florence. 129: From *A Suggestive Inquiry into Hermetic Philosophy and Alchemy* by Mary Anne South Atwood, Arno Press, New York, 1976. 130, 131: Andrew Clunies-Ross, Bournemouth—from *Agriculture of Tomorrow* by E. and L. Kolisko, Kolisko Archive, Bournemouth, England, 1978. 132-135: Courtesy Madame Jacqueline Barbault-Hattstatt. 137: Anglo-Australian Telescope Board.

Index

Numerals in italics indicate an illustration of the subject mentioned.

N

O

P

Q

R

S

T

U

V

W

X

Y

Z

TIME-LIFE BOOKS

EUROPEAN EDITOR: Ellen Phillips
Design Director: Ed Skyner
Director of Editorial Resources: Samantha Hill
Chief Sub-Editor: Ilse Gray
Assistant Design Director: Mary Staples

ISBN 0 7054 0693 8
TIME-LIFE is a trademark of Time Warner Inc. U.S.A.

MYSTERIES OF THE UNKNOWN

SERIES DIRECTOR: Jim Hicks
Series Administrator: Myrna Traylor-Herndon
Designer: Herbert H. Quarmby

Editorial Staff for *Secrets of the Alchemists*
Associate Editors: Susan V. Kelly (pictures); Robert A. Doyle (text)
Text Editor: Janet Cave
Researchers: Elizabeth Ward (principal), Patti H. Cass, Constance Contreras, Christian D. Kinney
Staff Writers: Margery A. duMond, Esther R. Ferington
Assistant Designer: Susan M. Gibas
Copy Coordinators: Colette Stockum, John Weber
Picture Coordinators: Michael Kentoff, Leanne G. Miller
Editorial Assistant: Donna Fountain

Special Contributors: Cheryl Binkley, Sheila M. Green, Patricia A. Paterno, Evelyn S. Prettyman (research); Norman S. Draper, Dónal Kevin Gordon, Lydia Preston Hicks, Harvey S. Loomis, Wendy Murphy, Bryce S. Walker, Danna L. Walker, Robert H. White (text); John Drummond (design); Hazel Blumberg-McKee (index).

Correspondents: Elisabeth Kraemer-Singh (Bonn), Christine Hinze (London), Christina Lieberman (New York), Maria Vincenza Aloisi (Paris), Ann Natanson (Rome). Valuable assistance was also provided by Mirka Gondicas (Athens); Tom Quinn (Bogotá); Angelika Lemmer (Bonn); Robert Kroon (Geneva); Bing Wong (Hong Kong); Judy Aspinall, Lesley Coleman (London); John Dunn (Melbourne); Sasha Isachenko, Felix Rosenthal (Moscow); Wibo van de Linde (the Netherlands); Meenakshi Ganguly (New Delhi); Elizabeth Brown (New York); Michael Donath (Prague); Ann Wise (Rome); Traudl Lessing (Vienna).

Consultants:
Marcello Truzzi, general consultant for the series, is a professor of sociology at Eastern Michigan University. He is also director of the Center for Scientific Anomalies Research (CSAR) and editor of its journal, the *Zetetic Scholar.* Dr. Truzzi, who considers himself a "constructive skeptic" with regard to claims of the paranormal, works through the CSAR to produce dialogues between critics and proponents of unusual scientific claims.

Joscelyn Godwin is a musicologist on the faculty of Colgate University who has made an extended study of esoteric philosophies and comparative religion. Among his published writings are studies of Renaissance scholars Robert Fludd and Athanasius Kircher, and translations of alchemical texts including *Splendor Solis* and *Atalanta Fugiens.*

Nathan Sivin is Professor of Chinese Culture and of the History of Science at the University of Pennsylvania. He is the author of *Chinese Alchemy: Preliminary Studies, Traditional Medicine in Contemporary China, Cosmos and Computation in Early Chinese Mathematical Astronomy,* and studies of many other aspects of science, medicine, and technology in East Asia.

This volume is one of a series that examines the history and nature of seemingly paranormal phenomena.

Colour reproduction by Liberty Engraving Co., Chicago, U.S.A.
Printed and bound by R.R. Donnelley & Sons Co., Willard, Ohio, U.S.A.